T0146874

SIX EVES PREVAIL

through the

Garden

of

NUTRITION

From the Campus to the
Conference Room

VERNELL E. STEWART BRITTON
LAURITA M. BURLEY
ANNIE B. CARR
FRANCES HANKS COOK
CATHERINE COWELL
WILMA ARDINE L. KIRCHHOFER

SIX EVES PREVAIL THROUGH THE GARDEN OF NUTRITION FROM THE CAMPUS TO THE CONFERENCE ROOM

iUniverse books may be ordered through booksellers or by contacting:

iUniverse
1663 Liberty Drive
Bloomington, IN 47403
www.iuniverse.com
1-800-Authors (1-800-288-4677)

Because of the dynamic nature of the Internet, any web addresses or links contained in this book may have changed since publication and may no longer be valid. The views expressed in this work are solely those of the author and do not necessarily reflect the views of the publisher, and the publisher hereby disclaims any responsibility for them.

Any people depicted in stock imagery provided by Thinkstock are models, and such images are being used for illustrative purposes only. Certain stock imagery © Thinkstock.

ISBN: 978-1-5320-0369-1 (sc)
ISBN: 978-1-5320-0370-7 (e)

Library of Congress Control Number: 2017900594

Print information available on the last page.

iUniverse rev. date: 05/03/2017

TABLE OF CONTENTS

PREFACE

$\mathcal{T}$his book evolved from a conversation had by a group of nutritionists in Atlanta, Georgia in 2012 during the visit of Catherine Cowell, retired Director of New York City's Bureau of Nutrition, Department of Public Health. They lamented the absence of public awareness of the small but vibrant array of professionally trained African American nutritionists in this country and agreed that something should be done about it. Writing a book was the next logical step. Of the original group of twenty women six remained to forge ahead, summarily enlisting a publisher, iUniverse and editor, Lydia Walker. Their stories necessarily pulled back important life curtains--drapes closed by the passage of time and the nature of progress. While each story is distinct, each demonstrates common core areas: family and family values; education and training, mentoring and service to the community.

DEDICATION

This book is dedicated to the memory of Mary Hollis Glenn, MA, RD, LD who was a member of the planning committee for this publication. A native Georgian, Glenn received a Bachelor of Science degree in Food, Nutrition and Institution Management from Savannah State College (now University) and completed a dietetic internship at Howard University in Washington, District of Columbia. In 1973 she became the first African American to be awarded the Master of Medical Science in Dietetics degree from Emory University, Atlanta, Georgia.

Glenn's professional career began as the Chief Dietitian for the Hughes Spalding Pavilion, a private hospital that served African American patients in Atlanta, Georgia before the integration of hospitals in Metro Atlanta. Over the next twenty-eight years, Glenn held several positions including nutrition coordinator of the Expanded Food and Nutrition Education Program and Teenage Mothers Nutrition Education Program with the University of Georgia DeKalb County Extension Service from which she retired in 2005.

Glenn was an accomplished leader with exceptional skills in organizational development. When Glenn solicited support for a project there was no way you could tell her "No" given her beautiful smile and infectious laughter. Her high level of commitment and participation did not go unnoticed; many awards and citations were bestowed: appointment to the first Georgia Board of Examiners for Licensed Dietitians by the Honorable Joe Frank Harris where she served as chairperson of the Board for two terms; first African American president of the Georgia Dietetic Association; named Georgia's Most Outstanding Dietitian in 1996; president of the Georgia Nutrition Council, the Morehouse School of Medicine National Black Leadership Initiative on Cancer and was Project Chair of the Congressional Black Caucus Foundation's Spirit of Healthy Living Program.

The Glenn family home was always steeped in religious faith, educational excellence and a commitment to service. Mary carried these gifts over into the community by serving as role model to generations of young people and was especially committed to helping develop their minds by demonstrating high moral and ethical standards. Her thirst for knowledge, her sense of humor, and her high regard for excellence are among her prized legacies. Mary Hollis Glenn departed this life February 1, 2013.

INTRODUCTION

SIX EVES PREVAIL through the GARDEN OF NUTRITION

$\mathcal{B}$e sure that you do not die without having done something wonderful for humanity. This caveat from the late Maya Angelou echoes the inspiration for what six Eves, aka registered female nutritionists call their Legacy Project. Legacy best describes the Eves' desire to create a body of work in the spirit of "giving back" to others what they have been blessed to achieve in the field of nutrition. In the words of Catherine Cowell, Ph.D. the most senior nutritionist among the Eves, "Giving back is the real measure and value of who you are and what you have learned concurrently with your unique skills."

The six nutritionists featured in this bio-flavored book dug deep into their individual patches of opportunity, planting seeds that sprouted like the fruit and veggies they would later advocate; ultimately blossoming into vine ripened professionals. The career paths of these spunky dietitian/nutritionists are at once different and the same. Like water in an irrigation pipeline the value of perseverance, intellectual curiosity and sacrifice flows through each story, backgrounds spanning New York City, Iowa and the South making no difference.

With experiences embracing children as well as adults, Eves also share funny anecdotes. Wilma Kirchhofer recalls the time she told a group of boys writing on the bus windows during a field trip, "Fool's names and fool's faces are often seen in public places." She left the bus for a few minutes and when she returned the boys had written "Mrs. K" on the windows. They couldn't spell Kirchhofer. Vernell Britton, not thinking about her "few extra pounds," told a 2nd grade class, "A nutritionist tells you how to eat well." "A little darling" then piped up, "You look like you eat well."

Laurita Burley had a similar encounter: a middle school lad looked at her poster display of food groups and asked, "Do you eat all the stuff you got up there?" Thinking food groups she replied, "I try to." The boy said, "No wonder you're so fat."

And no wonder Eves enjoyed the comic relief. Hard work was a given; perennial racism a common denominator. But like a garden's resilient succulents they weathered prickly weeds of injustice, rain sometimes torrential, and occasional drought. Taking their hands off the plow was never an option. Each Eve's story reveals courageous cultivation of the fertile academic soil that nourished their budding careers, ensuring personal growth and bounteous harvest.

Dr. Catherine Cowell, yet vibrant in the ninth decade of life can speak to the demanding lifestyle of the "well--trained professional dietitian." She implores her successors "to help improve the quality of life for all by giving generously of time, talent and skill in a setting that encircles respect of and sensitivity towards others." This book offers time-honored guidelines for doing that—and more! Welcome to the Garden of Nutrition.

Lydia Walker, Editor

I'LL BAKE THE CAKE

Vernell Stewart Britton

I joined the 4-H club and was the youngest member to attend the "short course" for 4-H'ers at Florida A&M University in Tallahassee, Florida. My interest in foods and nutrition began early. It was Mrs. Ethel Powell, who in later years teased me about always volunteering to bake the cake for any of our events. When the request for volunteers was made, she said I would raise my hand and say, "I'll bake the cake."

Many years later, I visited her when she was a resident of a nursing home in Jacksonville, Florida. She would ask me to push her around the facility in her wheelchair and as we approached the administrator or a director, she would introduce me to them and say to me, "Vernell, tell them what you do." I was thinking of replying that "I bake cakes," but I knew that she wanted everyone to know that I had an "important job." At that time, I was a regional nutrition consultant with the Division of Health Standards and Quality, Health Care Financing Administration and Florida was one of 8 states under our jurisdiction.

I met Mrs. Powell, a Home Demonstration Agent when I was a 6th grade student at Long Branch Elementary School in Jacksonville, Florida. She did not have biological children but was mentor/mother to many girls who were 4-H club members. My dear friend, Audrey Wilson Bowie called us "Mrs. Powell's girls." Mrs. Powell stressed the importance of doing good work and of being lady-like. She worked closely with us girls and our parents in a variety of community projects...gardening, cooking, canning, crafts, etc. We spent the night before trips at her home and would wake up early the following morning, have a warm glass of milk, and be on our way to Tampa for the state fair or some other city and event in Florida.

With Mrs. Ethel Powell

Always Look On the Bright Side

One of my mother's favorite sayings was "to look on the bright side." Perhaps these words have guided me on life's journey. The year was 1969. The girl from Jacksonville, Florida had just completed a dietetic internship. She was on her way to Milwaukee, Wisconsin to serve as a clinical dietitian at the Woods Veterans Administration Medical Center. Her thoughts were characterized by enthusiasm and anticipation of marvelous new experiences. I was that girl. My world was shaken that year by a "real life awakening." While members of my little village in

Jacksonville thought I was the "cream of the crop," and that anyone would be thrilled to have me as a neighbor, this view was not shared by the person who lived in the apartment above mine in Milwaukee.

Arriving in Milwaukee and settling into a cute apartment in a small complex across the street from the hospital, I was "on top of my world." But late at night and in the very early hours of the morning, I was awakened by loud banging and stomping by the person in the apartment above mine. As it was, this person did not want a Black person living in the building.

I was 21 years old and alone. I had no family or friends in the area. I was not comfortable living in a building with a person—"neighbor" with so much hate and bias in his heart that would cause him to use those tactics to harass and frighten me. I could have fought to stay in my apartment and was told that I would win, but I decided to move a few blocks away to another complex. The apartment was newer, had more amenities, and several professionals who worked at the VA lived there. Lessons learned from this experience: (1) There are some battles not worth fighting; (2) Timing is everything, (3) God alone is ruler over conscience, (4) Let go and live your life, (5) Don't allow others to steal your joy.

In the mid-seventies, I had a similar experience with housing in the Pelham Bay area in New York. I applied for an apartment, was approved but when the apartment manager learned that I was Black, the apartment was no longer available. This time, I decided to fight. My first thought was "how dare them" deny this apartment to me and approve someone who is not even employed. I was furious. Through a complaint with the New York Fair Housing Agency, an undercover person who was an unemployed white male was approved for the apartment. I "won" the case and the apartment was available for me. Again, I decided that I did not want to live in a building in which that type of bias and bigotry existed.

As I reflected on these two instances of discrimination in housing and other challenges in my life, I realized more fully the importance of having loving, supportive people in my life. My mother's advice to look on the bright side instilled in me the importance of focusing on the blessings of life and people and things that enhance your life. Hence, the village would forever shadow me.

My Parents and My First Village

I was very fortunate to have a loving and supportive mother and father, Willie and Maude Stewart who instilled in their children a sense of "who they were and whose they were." They worked hard all of their lives to provide opportunities for us that they did not have. I often think of them with admiration, love and respect for doing so much with their limited financial resources.

Me and my Parents, 1978

There were numerous members of the village, My Auntie/Moms (neighbors and friends as well as biological Aunts) who loved me and the other children in our neighborhood. To paint a picture of this village, it is necessary for me to give a glimpse of the remarkable women who comprised my first village. Their names were unique, few that you would hear today and, with few exceptions, they were called by their first names prefaced with "Ms." Responses to them ended with "ma'am, such as yes ma'am or no ma'am." They made the best fried chicken in the world, delicious cakes and pies, and seafood dishes. They sang songs, often with words that came to them as they sang. Their songs inspired us and made us laugh. These women, along with my mother were my first introduction to the world of food, its preparation, presentation, and enjoyment as well as to friendship and joy of life. I believe this first village set the tone for some very basics in my life. I knew that I was loved unconditionally and that I had the support of people who wanted the best for me. I knew that I could dream and pursue those dreams. They wanted me to have opportunities and options that had not been available to them. I loved them dearly, appreciated them more than they ever knew, and desired to make them proud. These words describe my feelings well. "It was somebody's teaching and praying that made a better person of me; of believing in me and thinking more highly of me than I deserved; that I knew I could not let them down."

The Meaning of Community in The 60's

On July 24, 1960, The Florida Times Union, the local newspaper in Jacksonville Florida featured an article, "Assembly and Contest by Local 4-H Club." This article was in the section of the newspaper designated as "News for and about Colored People." The article includes my name as narrator and the names of each student participant, teachers and parents who were either judges and/or supporters.

In reviewing this article two things became very clear. The first was the concept of community in those days and the manner in which everyone worked together for what was good for all of the children. As I read the name of each parent, most are not with us today. I said wow, this was the village; it just keeps extending. The section of the paper, "For and About Colored People" reflects the times in the 60's. The good news about "Colored People" appeared in a section designated for us.

1960 Florida Times Union Newspaper article
Assembly and Contest By Local 4-H Club

Early Influences: The Nutrition/Food Connection

It is important to note that nutritionists and dietitians are trained in the art and science of nutrition and are not trained to be cooks. I just happen to be a nutritionist who enjoys cooking and entertaining. Growing up in Jacksonville, I experienced numerous community events that centered on food and the presentation of marvelous culinary creations by people I admired and loved. I believe this was my inspiration to the joy of cooking. I observed my mother as she sectioned oranges for her ambrosia and would wait patiently for a taste. Seafood was a favorite and a special treat was her crab meat casserole. My godmother Edith's sour cream pound cake was also one of my favorites. During college years, she mailed care packages from Florida to Virginia which included one of those delicious cakes. Our neighbor, John Quarterman loved fishing and crabbing. He brought home huge crabs and brim fish, which are still my favorites.

The women in the community formed a social club and met monthly at each other's homes. When the meeting was at our home, there was a large array of food which included seafood salads, lovely garden salads, scrumptious desserts, and lots of warm fellowship and friendship. These events inspired me to cook and learn about recipes that made a delicious dish and that brought about fellowship, enjoyment and laughter. I began to experiment with different recipes and enjoyed sharing the finished dishes.

My God Mama's Sour Cream Pound Cake

½ pound of Butter
6 Eggs
3 cups of Sugar
3 cups of Plain Flour

½ pint of Sour Cream
¼ teaspoon of Baking Soda

Cream butter and sugar together. Add eggs two at a time, beating well after each addition. Beat until creamy. Sift flour and soda together. Alternately add the flour and sour cream to the mixture (butter, sugar, and egg mixture). Mix well. Pour batter into prepared (greased and floured) 10 inch tube pan. Bake at 300 F for 90 minutes or until cake tests done with a toothpick (The toothpick comes out clean when inserted into the cake).

Note: Start baking in a cold oven.
Servings: Approximately 20 slices
Nutrition Facts per Serving
Calories: 306.5
Fat: 12.7g
Protein: 4.8 g
Carbohydrates: 44.4 g
Cholesterol: 79.3 mg
Sodium: 106.9 mg
Sugar: 30.2 g

Mama's Crab Meat Casserole Revisited

My mama's crabmeat casserole was a family favorite. I have revised the recipe by replacing bread crumbs for the Ritz crackers that my mama used. Instead of the casserole, I make crab cakes.

Ingredients
1 pound of lump crab meat
1 small green pepper (¾ cup), diced
½ cup onions, chopped fine
2/3 cup bread crumbs

2 eggs, beaten
1 teaspoons of margarine
salt (optional)
pepper (optional)

Melt margarine. Sauté the green pepper and onions in melted margarine. In mixing bowl, combine the crab meat, the beaten eggs, and bread crumbs. Add the green pepper and onions. Mix all ingredients well. Add salt and pepper to taste. Heat 2 Tablespoons of olive oil in skillet. Shape the crab cake mixture into 2 ½ inch crab cakes. Cook in the hot oil until brown. Brown crab cakes on one side and then the other. This recipe makes about 6 crab cakes.

Nutrition Facts per Serving
Calories: 141
Calories from fat: 85
Total Fat: 9.5 g
Protein: 14.7 g
Carbohydrates: 11.4 g
Cholesterol: 97 mg
Sodium: 551 mg

As I gained knowledge through my high school home economics classes and my experiences with the 4-H club, I began to focus on nutrition. Interestingly, vegetables, fruits, and chicken were plentiful. The typical Sunday dinner was either fried or baked chicken with dressing, collard greens, rice, okra and tomatoes, macaroni and cheese and cornbread (a must with the greens). Dessert was usually a homemade pound cake and Jell-O with fruit. We had dinner after church and of course, the food would be there for eating all day. I talked to my mother about the dinner menus. For example, minimizing starchy items and using less sugar in homemade iced tea or lemonade. My older brother began to tease me about my unsweetened beverages.

Rice was a staple in our home. Regardless of the menu, it included rice. I was very fascinated by the way the food was presented and beautiful table settings. While I took care in the preparation of a dish, I also took great care in presenting a beautiful table. I won first prize in my first baking competition. I made muffins. I simply followed my mother's advice that the key was to cream the sugar and margarine very well. I also won a trip to Washington, DC to attend a national 4-H meeting.

This connection between food and nutrition became clearer as I gained experience and knowledge; I knew that nutrition and healthy eating were interrelated and important. As a clinical dietitian in a hospital setting, I was able to coordinate the planning of nutritionally adequate menus based on specific dietary restrictions. I used my training and nutrition knowledge in teaching patients and families and in offering expert opinion to members of the health care team regarding overall patient care.

Later as a public health nutritionist and one of the first surveyors in Florida, I monitored nutritional care in health care facilities and made recommendations regarding standards for nutritional care for residents in health care facilities. My work in this area expanded to the regional level that included the New York region, the Southeast, and nationally.

The Impact of Early Teachers

My elementary and high school teachers were very instrumental in my life. My 2nd grade teacher brought cereal and milk for our morning snack (at that time there was not a cafeteria in our school). She told us not to add sugar. This habit stayed with me for life. My 6th grade teacher, Ms. Sylvia Mungen, took me under her wings and provided extensive support, coaching, and encouragement. When I hear the song, "Sweet, Sweet Spirit," I think of her. She was the greatest teacher! She had a way of making all of her students feel special. Ms. Mungen lost a leg in a car accident and faced many challenges in getting to school (at that time modifications for disabilities were not in place at our elementary school). Later, when a cafeteria/auditorium was added I would often go to the cafeteria and get my lunch or beverage and stay in the classroom with her.

I played the role of Aunt Drusilla in the school's operetta, Aunt Drusilla's Garden. During one of the rehearsals, I hit a wrong note in my solo; some kids giggled. After that, I decided that I was not going to be in the operetta. This decision was made solely by me, an 11 year old. None of the teachers or my parents knew anything about this decision. So when I entered the area one day during rehearsal and was asked by the teacher/director why I was not at rehearsal, I simply replied, "Oh, I am not going to be in it." Needless to say, once teachers and parents conferred, I was back at rehearsal and the star of the operetta.

Career Choices

In Jacksonville, I attended Matthew W. Gilbert, an all-black high school. I do not remember any discussion regarding career choices, things you were "good at," your interests, etc. I remember that many of my senior classmates listed nursing and teaching as their ambition. I did not want to go into either of these fields. So, I made several visits to our school library to research careers--those related to home economics, food, etc. I came across the career of hospital dietetics. Interestingly in my senior yearbook, I listed a "career in the field of home economics" as my career preference. Perhaps I wanted to consider the various options in this field.

Reflecting on my decision, I realize that it was just perfect for me. My career has taken me to positions in all parts of the US and in a variety of settings. The early years as a dietitian in a hospital setting set a strong foundation in clinical as well as administrative areas of dietetics. Because I was single and adventurous, I took advantage of opportunities in the field of nutrition. When I would hear about a new position, I would reply, "That sounds interesting." So it is no surprise that my journey took me to several regions of our country.

Hampton University: My Home by the Sea

"Oh Hampton we never can make thee a song, except as our lives do the singing. In service that will, thou great spirit prolong and send it through centuries ringing."

I entered Hampton University in 1961. I was apprehensive about how I would fit in this "new world." Until then, my world was a small, very protective, nurturing and supportive community in Jacksonville, Florida. Other than trips throughout Florida and the trip I won to Washington, DC., my travels were limited. During my first semester, I enrolled in a physical science class. I remember the professor, a big man strutting in the classroom and saying, "I know that most of you come from these communities where you were the cream of the crop, the apple of everyone's eye, the center of attention, but here at Hampton, you are one over 1900," meaning 1/1900. Nineteen hundred was the number of students at that time. I gasped. This professor actually turned out to be one of the gentlest, kindest persons, but he surely took the wind out of my sails on that first day.

I joined Alpha Kappa Alpha Sorority and had a very close, supportive circle of friends. I had the same roommate for all four years of college. We remained friends until her death in 2008. I remember fretting about my organic chemistry final exam and one of my sorors insisted that I give it my best. With her help, I studied late into the night and was able to do well on the exam.

With sorors at Hampton University in 1963

While at Hampton, I worked during one summer for the city hospitals of New York-- a great salary for a college student and a good experience. After graduation, I returned to New York and worked as a staff dietitian at one of the city hospitals. I worked on weekends and would often have to open units. It seemed as if every weekend many of the workers would call in sick and it was very challenging to make the schedule changes that were needed for optimal food service to the patients. I decided early that this was not for me and began applying for dietetic internships. I was accepted at internships in Poughkeepsie, New York and in Cleveland, Ohio. I chose Cleveland because it was a coordinated internship/Master's degree program.

My Internship: One of Those Necessary Bends in the Road

The internship program was coordinated among Case Western Reserve University and three hospitals--Cleveland Veterans Administration Medical Center, Mt. Sinai Hospital, and University Hospital. I was assigned to the Cleveland Veterans Administration Medical Center. There were 17 in the program, 2 of us African American. Our internship director at the VA was Joan Kanjuck. She was supportive and made us feel at ease. I was impressed by her treatment of us interns as professionals. Our class was the second in the coordinated program and the programs overlapped. Members of the first class became our "big sisters." My big sister was Vicki Bowie from Texas. She was beautiful, smart, and wise.

My experiences at the VA are most memorable while those in the nutrition department at Case Western were not as positive; I always felt that I was not treated fairly. I remember working very hard on an essay, only to receive a C+. I was so hurt and so very disappointed. The professor remained a challenge and I realized that whatever I did would not be exceptional to her. So, I simply did my best, which is all that I could do. Again that solid foundation gained from my first village in Jacksonville played again and again in my ear, reminding me of who I am and whose I am.

Entering the doors of the VA Medical Center in Cleveland and into the warm, welcoming dietetics department, I felt accepted and encouraged. I worked closely with the administrative dietitian, Mrs. Carrie Harris, the ultimate professional who was warm and caring, supportive, and candid. I remember her telling me to keep my hairnet on. I had a habit of taking it off as soon as I left the kitchen area. Another time, when I was dismayed by what I perceived as "unfair treatment" by a professor at Case Western Reserve University, Mrs.

Harris reminded me, "When you receive your master's degree and apply for a job, no one is going to ask you about that professor." That one statement had a significant impact on me. I began to focus less on the professor and more on learning and just doing my best. I realized that I had to forget about "fairness." The concept of fairness is an interesting topic for discussion; a former colleague once said that she told her children that fairness rarely exists. If you get it, be very grateful, but always try to give it/use it in your dealings with others. She was quite a wise lady.

The dietary employees at the VA took pride in their jobs and were extremely helpful and kind to the interns. They willingly shared their skills and their knowledge. I remember the baker who carefully taught us how to operate the various pieces of equipment. In those days, everything was prepared on site. I also remember one food service worker who was responsible for salad preparation stating that if we were not careful, the sinks would be the healthiest things around us. She was alluding to the fact that we should be careful not to let the salad greens soak in the water for long periods.

While the employees were champions of all the interns, I always felt that they had a special sense of pride for Kay Booker, the other African American intern and me. Many of them would offer words of encouragement that made difficult times bearable. I still think of them fondly and with immense gratitude for making those experiences such a wonderful part of my journey in the profession of Nutrition.

Why Are We Here

When I became manager of a Branch with survey responsibilities and some staff members were not performing as I thought they should,

I made the statement to a colleague, "Why do they think they are here?" She jokingly replied "to have fun" and we both laughed. It was a good laugh, but this one question has been a guiding factor in all of my work. Why am I here? Throughout all of my work experiences, I am so grateful that I have been able to answer this question and to focus on the people served. While not always easy, I believe the ability to weave through the people and things that get in the way of serving others, of knowing our true purpose is very valuable.

My Patients: The Veterans

I spoke earlier of the importance of food presentation. At the VA, we periodically conducted patient surveys regarding the menus. One menu consisted of baked chicken, cauliflower, and mashed potatoes. My evaluation was that it was too bland in color. However, the patients did not care about the color; this was one of their favorite meals. So we added garnishes for a more attractive presentation.

My experience at the VA made me more sensitive and appreciative of our veterans. One of my assignments was on the spinal cord injury unit. I met many young men returning from Vietnam with horrendous injuries, but who maintained extraordinary spirits and pride of country that would make anyone proud. I had a reputation of "spoiling them" and I was guilty. They got pretty much what they wanted within dietary guidelines. One of the most meaningful parts of my day was to make rounds at meal times and visit with them. I often think of these patients and wonder where their journeys have taken them. Another memory is of our assignment on the renal dialysis unit. As we entered the area, one by one, an intern would faint (I think there were four of us on the unit at the time). I was concerned that I would be the next to faint. Thankfully, I did not. Later, the dietitian told us that the fainting was probably related to the warm temperature in the room combined with seeing blood flowing through the tubes.

My First American Dietetic Association (ADA) Meeting (now Food Nutrition Conference & Expo) Carl Stokes, the Mayor of Cleveland, Ohio

During my internship, the American Dietetic Association (now the Academy of Nutrition and Dietetics) held its national meeting in Cleveland. One of the welcome addresses at the opening ceremony was given by Carl Stokes, the first Black Mayor of Cleveland. I was very impressed and beamed with pride as he spoke. Many years later while living in New York, my husband and I had dinner with Carl and his wife at their home in the city. He and my husband had been friends for many years. Carl was a news anchor at NBC. It was a delightful evening and I shared with him my story about the ADA meeting in Cleveland. Indeed, life is filled with wonderful memories.

Church Made a Difference

Growing up in Jacksonville, church was a part of our life. There was never a question as to whether we would attend or not attend. We knew that on Sundays, we would attend Sunday school, morning worship, and scheduled afternoon activities. This was a time for learning, for fellowship, and enjoyment. We enjoyed going to church. So it is no surprise that this habit followed me wherever I went. While an intern in Cleveland, I attended Mt. Zion Congregational Church. I loved going to this church. The Minister, Rev. Andrews delivered messages that were very meaningful and practical. His wife, Marjorie was the organist at the church at one time. I thought the music was simply beautiful. I still have one of her albums, *Behold, Now Praise the Lord*, that was given to me by Rev. Andrews.

Whenever I talked to Rev Andrews about my challenges, frustrations, hurt, and disappointments during my internship experiences, he provided words of wisdom and encouragement. He was my father figure in Cleveland. He took the time to really listen to my spoken words as well as those unspoken. I remember in a discussion about relationships, he made the statement, "Women are like roses. They should be treated lovingly and gently. If you bruise one petal, you bruise the entire rose." I have never forgotten that statement.

The Village Continues: My Family in Cleveland

Victoria McAdoo and her family lived in Cleveland and were dear friends of one of my mentors in Jacksonville. I was given instructions to call her when I arrived in Cleveland. That was the best advice ever. The McAdoo family became my family in Cleveland. Rev. McAdoo was minister of a Lutheran church in Cleveland and Vicki was a schoolteacher. They had two daughters and a son. I visited them on weekends and stayed for dinner on Sundays. Vicki checked on me regularly and brought treats when she thought I needed them. She is the epitome of genuine love and caring. We still communicate and exchange cards on special occasions. I always send her a Mother's Day greeting because she is one of the many wonderful "mothers" who enhanced my life in immeasurable ways. Again, I went to Cleveland not knowing anyone but was embraced by this wonderful, loving family. They became the focal point of love and support. I talked with Vicki about my challenges and she listened and provided guidance.

My "Cleveland, Ohio Family" Vicki McAdoo and children, 1966

The Woods Veterans Administration Hospital and New Friendships

My first job after the dietetic internship was as staff dietitian at the Veterans Administration Medical Center (VMAC) in Milwaukee, Wisconsin. My internship director and administrative dietitian at the Cleveland VAMC encouraged me to apply for and accept the job offer as clinical dietitian in Milwaukee. They believed that under the dynamic leadership of Frances and Eileen (Kelley and Kelly, Chief and Assistant Chief of Dietetic Service), I would get remarkable experience both in the clinical and the administrative areas. Indeed, they were correct. The dietary department was well-organized with the most proficient staff. The kitchen had all new stainless steel, state of the art equipment and was always immaculate. While the work experience was exceptional, once more I encountered problems with housing.

As a clinical dietitian at the Woods Veterans Administration
Medical Center, Milwaukee, Wisconsin 1969

I took it for granted that I would live in the area near the hospital and
never imagined any problems because of my race. I was mistaken.
I found myself moving from one apartment to another. As it is
often said, "when one door closes another one opens." At my new
apartment, I met Cathy Stehr, a physical therapist and Donna
Schmidt, a pharmacist. We became close friends and that friendship
was a source of joy and fun during my year in Milwaukee. We
prepared dinner and shared with each other weekly. This was a time
when I particularly enjoyed experimenting with recipes.

I met Bettie Givens, a dietitian at another hospital in Milwaukee.
Bettie became my special friend and I spent many weekends with her
and her family. I also became friends with a nurse, Inadelle Crawford
at the VA. She and her young sons visited me when I moved to
Florida. More than twenty years later our paths crossed again and it
was a great time to reconnect after so many years.

Home Sweet Home: Working In My Home State

Milwaukee was much too cold for this Florida girl. After spending a year in Milwaukee, I moved back home to Jacksonville, Florida and began work as a nutritionist with the Department of Health and Rehabilitative Services under the leadership of Mildred Kaufman, the State's head nutritionist. Along with Marge Knapp and Mamie Davis, I was a state nutritionist who conducted surveys of health care facilities throughout the state. This was at the time when many of the nursing homes were referred to as the mom and pop operations, basically because of the physical facility as well as the type of operations. With the enforcement of life safety code regulations and the advances in State and Federal regulations, I witnessed significant changes, particularly in the area of long term care. If we take a walk back in history from the late 1960's to the present, we would see a significant decline in the number of injuries and deaths related to building and code violations. This is a significant outcome of enforcement of codes and regulations.

After returning to my home state, I became very active with the professional organization and was elected president of the Jacksonville Dietetic Association. I was also very active in training programs for Food Service Supervisors. Because this was home, I was often requested to speak to community groups on various topics.

1971 Florida Times Union news article
Food demonstration at public library
Jacksonville, FL

Be Sure To Wear a Flower in Your Hair

I arrived in Berkeley, California in 1971 without any job prospects. A dear friend, Dorene Carter, a native of St. Croix, US Virgin Islands, was in the nutrition doctoral program at the University of California in Berkeley. She and I met in Cleveland during my internship (she was a graduate student at Case Western Reserve University). With a spirit of excitement, adventure and a desire to live in California, I made the move. I did not have a care or concern about finding work.

I was encouraged by Dorene. She and another soon to be friend, Lula Greene, and I rented a 3-bedroom apartment in Berkeley and thus began another marvelous journey. My mentors in Florida had given me the names of nutritionists to contact for help with finding suitable work. One of the first calls I made was to Doris Lauber, a public health nutritionist, who gave me several job leads. With her help, I was able to start work in a very short period of time. My first job, part time and temporary, was to assist a graduate student with data for one of her projects. I also began two part-time positions. The first was as nutritionist at a Children and Youth project at Mt. Zion Hospital in San Francisco. In this position, I taught nutrition classes to pregnant teenagers and worked with mothers and their babies in the well-child clinic. The other was as a part time nutritionist at the health department in Vallejo, California. Everything worked out perfectly. I loved driving from Berkeley to Vallejo, two or three days per week, providing nutrition consultation to patients in the clinic and interacting with other members of the health care team. In less than a year, the job at Mt. Zion became fulltime and I was selected as the Chief of Nutrition Services.

The relationships and lifelong friendships developed during these years are ones that still bring back wonderful memories and smiles. I remember this as a time of tremendous fun. Weekends included brunch at local restaurants, bike rides at Golden Gate Park, and walks through Hilden Park in Berkeley. On one of my return trips from Florida, I was met at the airport in San Francisco by my friends and driven to a concert featuring Marvin Gay and Ashford and Simpson. It was a fabulous evening. Other favorite memories include trips to Lake Tahoe and Reno, of parties and dinners celebrating our birthdays and special occasions, and of glorious laughter and joy. The lyrics, "When you come to San Francisco, be sure to wear a flower in your hair" fit this city and time of my life.

Laughing Out Loud While At Carmel by the Sea

As I look back on my career, I can smile and laugh about parts of the journey. These are wonderful memories. The time in California was truly fun. One day six of us got into my green Camaro and headed from San Francisco to Carmel. Along this beautiful drive, we sang and laughed. Arriving in Carmel, we enjoyed the magnificent views, took pictures and just had a joyous time. We had dinner at a fabulous restaurant with picturesque views of the cliffs and Monterey Bay.

On the way to Carmel By The Sea with friends
Audrey Wilson and Phyllis Stubbs, 1973

New York, New York…Again

After three years in California, I moved to New York City and began work as a public health nutritionist with the New York State Department of Health in the White Plains Regional Office. This was after a month with the City of New York in which I did not receive a salary. In White Plains, I worked with a team of nutritionists under the leadership of Beth Lund. Diane Philips, one of the nutritionists and I became friends and remain friends today. We were responsible for conducting surveys of health facilities. The work was enjoyable and we were very fond of each other. This, combined with Beth being an exceptional leader made the years in White Plains very memorable.

A friend, Robbie Graham, who was chief dietitian at the VA Medical Center in the Bronx, New York told me about a job opening with the Federal government, specifically the Department of Health and Human Services in the New York regional office. I remember completing the application while I was attending a 6 week surveyor training program at Tulane University in Louisiana. I mentioned this to a fellow attendee who was a Federal employee in the Seattle regional office. She advised me to pay close attention in responding to questions relating to Knowledge, Skills, and Abilities (KSAs). She stated that the information was reviewed by personnel staff who looked for key words. So I was very careful and included detail about all related experiences and education.

I applied for the job, was selected as the regional nutritionist, and was on a three- member team consisting of two nurses and myself. I enjoyed this experience, especially with the program and operations staff that made jokes about me, their nutritionist. I often baked goodies for the staff and a favorite was zucchini bread. At one of the annual holiday celebrations, a picture was drawn on a poster with a green blob indicating me and zucchini.

It was during my second stint in New York that I met Elizabeth Siegel, a nutrition consultant in the White Plains region. Although there was about a 20 year difference in our ages, we became close friends. Elizabeth was a very petite, classy lady with outstanding culinary skills. I enjoyed immensely having dinner with her and her husband in New York City as well as having lunch with her in many quaint and fabulous restaurants in the city. We spent many

Saturdays walking down Madison Ave browsing in shops, chatting, and simply enjoying the city. It was Elizabeth who taught me how to make the best crab salad, emphasizing that the quality of the crabmeat was the key. She shared some of her favorite recipes with me in a book, *Recipe Collectors Notebook*. All of the recipes were handwritten by her and are still among my favorites.

Zucchini Bread

3 Eggs
1 cup of Oil (I use canola oil)
1 ¾ cups of Sugar
2 cups of grated, unpeeled Raw Zucchini
2 teaspoons of Ground Cinnamon
1 teaspoon of Salt
1 teaspoon of Baking Soda
¼ teaspoon of Baking Powder
3 cups of unsifted Flour
1 cup of Chopped Walnuts

Beat eggs in large bowl until foamy. Gradually beat in oil and sugar. Add grated zucchini, cinnamon, salt, baking soda, and baking powder. Mix well. Gradually add flour, blending well after each addition. Fold in chopped walnuts. Pour mixture in to a prepared (greased and floured) 10 inch tube pan or two 8x4 loaf pans. Bake in 350 degree oven for one hour or until bread tests done and begins to leave the sides of the pan. Cool in pan for 10 minutes. Loosen edge and turn bread on rack to continue cooling. Wrap in foil or placed in covered cake container for storage.

Approximately 16 servings
Nutrition Facts Per Serving
Calories: 355.2

Total Fat: 19.9 g
Proteins: 5.2 g
Carbohydrates: 40.6 g
Cholesterol: 31.8 mg
Sodium: 182.7 mg
Sugar: 22.7g

Atlanta, Georgia

Leaving New York for Atlanta was easy. Although I knew I would miss my friends, I believed that the friendships would remain regardless of where I lived. One dear friend in New York, Eldridge Greenlee, gave me a card with the following note: "Vernell, you have to have it all. Anyone who can leave California for New York and leave New York for Atlanta has to have it all. I will require frequent visits for the price of letting you go."

In Atlanta's office of Health Standards and Quality in the US Department of Health and Human Services, I was welcomed by the same professionalism, efficiency, fun-loving spirit as I had experienced in New York. I joined a large team of several nurses, social workers, pharmacists, administrative surveyors, and life safety code inspectors. I was the only nutritionist and the first Black surveyor on this team. I was in the South and our state assignments were Alabama, Florida, Georgia, Kentucky, Mississippi, North Carolina, South Carolina, and Tennessee.

The first letter I received was from Mendel Kemp, Director of Survey and Certification in the State of Mississippi who welcomed me to the region and to his state. Working in Mississippi was an absolutely marvelous experience. I developed a very close working relationship with the nutritionists in the eight states with licensure and survey responsibilities and gained the utmost respect of the survey team members and state leaders. I remember traveling with the Mississippi State nutritionist, conducting surveys and training programs throughout the State. We arrived in one location and my room was upgraded. She teased me for the rest of the trip on how well Mississippi treated me. While my colleagues in the region and in the states were very welcoming, this was not always the case with hotel reservationists and restaurant personnel in the various states.

Often, when the hotel clerks would assign a room to me far away from the other team members, one of the men in our group would take my room and give me theirs. If we were out to dinner or lunch and I was not treated well, the entire team would leave. Because we travelled often, we became good friends as well as colleagues. The friendships never "got in the way" of the work. We worked hard, but enjoyed our work. We supported each other and represented our agency well. These years are among the most rewarding of my career not only because of the accomplishments made but also because the people were first-class professionals.

Washington, DC and Atlanta, Georgia

While in Atlanta, I married Theodore R. Britton, Jr. who had served as US Ambassador to Barbados. After our marriage, we moved to Washington, DC where my husband served as Under Secretary for International Affairs with the Department of Housing and Urban Development (HUD). This is where my international exposure blossomed as we were guests at various embassies and events in Washington and hosted many groups from other countries. This is when I attended my first inaugural ball. Ronald Reagan was President.

One of the first groups we entertained in our home in Washington, DC was a group from China. I welcomed the ladies into the kitchen as I prepared various dishes. They had a marvelous time and insisted on helping. We developed great friendships. Later when we visited China, it was like meeting old friends again.

My husband is a "people person" and never meets a stranger, so every place we visited, he had a friend. I remember a trip to Arcadia National Park in Maine. He called Warren Lindquist, a friend who lived in Seal Harbor. Warren invited us and our two nieces to his home where he prepared and taught the girls how to eat lobster. Our travels took us to various parts of France, The United Kingdom, Mexico, Japan, Germany, Spain, Italy, South Africa, Peru, Austria, Australia, Belgium, Canada, parts of Scandinavia, South Korea, China and the Caribbean. While my husband's travel experiences were vast (he has travelled to more than 167 countries), my travel had not been as extensive. We were fortunate to have the opportunity to travel for work, with People to People International, and various personal travels. I found it fascinating to experience meals around the world and was able to share and learn from others. One of the outstanding meals was in a little restaurant in Woodstock, England. Every item was prepared to perfection and the presentation was exquisite. On a trip to Paris, we found a very small neighborhood restaurant that was filled, but the owner removed some items from a small table to accommodate my husband, our friend, Betty Scott, and me. The meal and the people were fabulous and our evening was just as fabulous.

Train ride with my husband from Xian to Beijing

Boat ride on the River Seine, Paris France with my husband and Friends

Return to Atlanta

I returned to Atlanta in 1983 and again joined the office of Health Standards and Quality in region 4. Later, I was promoted to the position of Branch Manager. This experience was extremely rewarding. At that time, I was able to select the largest group of surveyors, primarily nurses in the history of the organization. My boss, Clarence Boone, the Associate Regional Administrator told me that I had done an outstanding job of selecting the individuals, coordinating the training, and acclimating them into the organization. Many of these individuals became leaders in the organization.

The organization changed names from the Health Care Financing Administration (HCFA) to the Centers for Medicare and Medicaid Services (CMS). I transferred from the Division of Health Standards and Quality to the Division of Medicaid and retired in 2006 as manager of Medicare Outreach and Education in the Division of Medicare.

The Atlanta Project

An article appeared in the Atlanta Journal and Constitution about a baby in the neonatal unit at Grady Hospital and President Jimmy Carter's vision to connect what he referred to as the "Two Atlantas." One was the Atlanta with tremendous opportunities and resources while the other was the Atlanta with tremendous needs and limited resources. The Atlanta Project was organized around cluster communities, each with a corporate sponsor and an emphasis on community involvement. I volunteered in the area of Health and was granted a 3-month detail by my employer to work as the assistant to the secretariat for health. This experience was extremely rewarding because I was able to work directly with people, use my creative skills and see the results of our efforts. The number of individuals who were members of our volunteer force was impressive. Again, I was touched by the outpouring of support from ordinary people who simply wanted to help others. While some of our goals were reached, many programs and projects made a difference in the targeted communities.

With President Carter Atlanta Project Reception

The Building of Skills

There comes a point in life when you realize that you are really good at some things. For me, it was the realization that I am very good at analyzing situations, finding solutions, and communicating issues and possible solutions to others. I see this as a result of the many years I spent at the State and Federal governmental agencies as nutrition consultant.

I genuinely care for people regardless of positon, title, perceived status, etc. My former pastor commented to me that my genuine caring and ability to connect with people was a special gift. I know that these gifts, these skills are the result of many people over many years who worked with me in every aspect of doing a job well. My mother always told us how special we were. She would also say that others were not "better than us" and we "were not better than others," so as to teach us to look highly on ourselves while not "looking down on others." This may also be one of the reasons I always related to the phrase, "to walk with Kings and not lose the common touch" in Kipling's "If" as well as the words in "Myself" by Edgar Guest.

With my husband Ted Britton and fellow
"Eves" writer, Catherine Cowell, 1992

Some of My Favorite Things

Some of my favorite things to do are to meet our friend, Bernard Pin in Paris and enjoy an evening of dining and fellowship and to take our friend, Genci Mucaj from Albania to have his favorite lamb dish prepared by Chef Wendy at the former Eurasia Restaurant in Decatur, GA. I enjoy travelling with my husband and the continuous history lessons. And of course, my nieces and nephews are a source of fun and joy. They make me smile. With them, I continue to learn and experience again and again the special joy of loving children and being stretched beyond my wildest imagination in the capacity to love.

I enjoy time with my friends and entertaining them in our home. My husband and I have hosted several international groups in our home. What I have found is that people all over the world are "some kind of wonderful" if we simply take the time to get to know one another. Often, we think we are the teachers, but I have found that we can learn a great deal from others. Mealtimes provide wonderful opportunities to get to know others and to demonstrate a little of what nutrition entails.

Coping With Loss

I was 36 when my Mother died and I thought I would never stop crying. I remember telling my best friend that I would be able to handle anything after this, because it was not possible for anything to hurt worse than this. Of course this was not true. When I lost her, my best friend, Audrey Wilson Bowie, I again thought I would never stop crying. And those seemingly endless tears were also shed for my daddy, sisters, brothers, cousins, aunts, nephews, other family members and friends. Our immediate family which was at one time a large circle of people is becoming a close-knit arc.

Happy Times with my dear friend, Audrey

I lost both of my sisters to cancer. My youngest sister, Meriel was a breast cancer survivor for six years. She died in 2005. My oldest sister, Gloria died of lung cancer in 2007. In 2013, I lost an older brother, Nathaniel and my only surviving aunt (my mother's oldest sister). Our immediate family is now 2 brothers, one older and one younger and me.

Several things have helped me cope with the losses. Words from a former pastor have proven true; you cannot repay them for the part they played in your life, for the love and experiences. But you can pass that love on to others. The other is that we honor them by living life, by enjoying the moments, by sharing and giving to others in ways that would make them smile. So as a dear friend often tells me that perhaps "we are here for such a time as this," I am encouraged and inspired to be of service to others. I became the Auntie/Mom of my sister Meriel's son, Teron. He is now a senior at Hampton University. I also became the founder of Meriel's Miracles, a 501c3 organization in memory of my youngest Sister. The mission of the organization is to support children in families affected by cancer. I retired from the Centers for Medicare and Medicaid Services (CMS) in 2006. I am currently employed as a nutrition auditor with Atlanta Public Schools.

With my youngest sister, Meriel and her son, Teron.

A Special Thank You to My Village

I have been very fortunate to have met many wonderful people who have been a part of my life's journey. Each person has been a part of this beautiful patchwork that has enhanced my life in immeasurable ways. Nutrition has been my life passion, starting with that small village of women in Jacksonville, Florida. I learned to grasp each moment, each opportunity, to give of my best, and to treat others well. It was my intent to demonstrate the importance of people in our lives and how each experience adds to the total joy.

My heartfelt thanks are extended to my village which continues to grow and enrich my life's journey. I seek to be a part of a village for others and pass on the support and love I have been blessed to experience. Writing my story has afforded me the opportunity to reflect on my village, rekindling my desire to share my time, talent and truth with others.

Lessons Learned/This I Know...

Some life lessons I would like to share especially with young people who are making career choices, and simply trying to make sense "of it all."

- Seize opportunities to learn and grow ... never stop learning.
- All human beings are first class citizens . . . Treat them that way.
- Find your passion, the work that brings you joy and "go with it."
- Do your best every day, in every way.

In the words of our dear friend, the late Ethelin Jarvis, "Honey, you just build memories."

You Might as Well Be a Doctor

Laurita Burley

*I*t was about 5:00 am on a late May morning in 1953. The school year had ended and my parents had carefully packed the trunk of our Ford with boxes of Mason jars filled with peaches, string beans, field peas, and what we called "soup mix," a blend of corn, okra and tomatoes. In addition to the home-canned goods, there were enough clothes, bedding and other small household items to last through two summer sessions of graduate school at Tuskegee Institute (now University).

Barely tall enough to see the roadside from the back seat, I gazed sleepily from the window as we passed newly planted cotton fields, tall pine trees and grazing cattle. I watched my father move the gear stick on the steering column up and down, back and forth, as we poked toward city limit signs and in less than two miles, back onto two-lane highways heading westward toward Alabama. It was an exciting time. The town of Tuskegee had little more to offer than the small Georgia town where we lived, but on campus there was the Chambliss Children's House where I would attend summer school, and the children's reading room in the campus library, summer concerts and other activities.

Most stories about professional achievements and African Americans describe aspirations rooted in determination to escape poverty, yearning for occupational mobility (as was the case for my parents), and navigating hurdles of racism. My story, however, is not so much about racism, though it obviously existed, but about how my parents, community and a black college prepared me for a world outside of their protection. I never gave much thought to my motive for attending college. I simply knew that I was going.

Beginnings

Growing up as an African American in the segregated rural southern United States, I was fortunate to have parents who were educators, and in addition conscientious teachers who wanted the best for me, and demanded that I do my best. My mother was a high school home economics teacher and was certified in elementary education, but I never enrolled in any of her classes. At home, I listened and observed as she carefully prepared meals with my father's special dietary needs in mind. Except for baked goods, foods were prepared simply. Besides, our small town grocer did not stock a wide variety of herbs and exotic spices. Generally, she followed a pattern of meat, vegetable and a starch. My father detested margarine so she used real butter and occasionally bacon drippings. The issue of saturated versus *trans* fat had not become a public health concern. He merely complained that margarine was artificial and did not taste good. Early on, I learned that some health conditions require watching what or changing the way you eat. Although I did not know about dietetics, this was perhaps my earliest introduction. What followed was an adventure of discovering the profession and defining my place in it.

Basic Sweet Rolls

(From my mother's handwritten copy)

2 pkgs. dry yeast
1 Tablespoon sugar
½ cup warm water
1 cup flour
3 eggs
½ cup evaporated milk
½ cup butter, melted
1 ½ teaspoons salt
½ cup sugar
4-5 cups flour

Sprinkle yeast and 1 Tablespoon sugar over warm water in large bowl. When sugar and yeast have been dissolved, add 1 cup of flour; beat well and set aside until sponge forms. In another bowl beat eggs well; add evaporated milk, cooled butter, salt and sugar. Mix and add all at once to sponge. Add enough flour to make soft dough, about 3-4 cups. Turn dough out on floured board and knead until smooth and elastic. Use remaining flour as needed to prevent dough from sticking to the board. Do not add too much flour!

Place dough in greased bowl and brush top with melted butter. Cover with damp cloth and let dough rise until double in bulk, approximately 1 to 1 ½ hours; knead down. Shape into desired shapes. Allow to double in bulk again and then bake in hot oven, 400⁰, 12-15 minutes.

Note: This dough may be used for any of the following forms of rolls: Bowknot, Crescent, Clover Leaf, Butterhorn, Layer, Parker House and Cinnamon; also Coffee Cakes and Braids.

Makes 2 dozen rolls.

Nutrition Facts per serving (one roll)

Calories 150.9, Fat 5.8 g, Saturated Fat 3.1g, Trans Fat 0.25g, Carbohydrate 20.0 g, Fiber 0.85, Protein 4.6 g, Sodium 188.9 mg, Cholesterol 36.2 mg

I was the only child when my parents graduated from college and in 1952 when they moved from Tuskegee, Alabama to accept teaching positions in rural Georgia. They did not find childcare right away, so at age four I began attending public school. My classroom was the nave of a small wooden church. The setting was the classic one often depicted in stories about one-room schoolhouses. Near the front of the room was a table with a bench for sitting on each side. In the center of the room was a potbelly stove, the only source of heat during the winter. Off to the side, and underneath a window sat a small table lined with cups, glasses, and a dipper that hung on the side of a metal bucket filled with drinking water drawn from a faucet that stood alone in the church yard. Because of my age, I could not enroll in school. Nevertheless, the teacher, Mrs. Jones, allowed me to sit at the table with other children.

According to my report card, before the school term ended I was classified "1A." Perhaps that would have been the equivalent of what we now call pre-K had it existed back then. The promotion would have meant a move down the narrow unpaved street to the school where the campus consisted of one wooden building, tarpapered barracks and two latrines, converted surplus from a nearby airbase and remnants from World War II. In 2016, I had the pleasure of speaking with Mrs. Gladys Cordy, my "pre-K" (and later first-grade) teacher. During our telephone conversation she reminded me that we went to the "cow pen" building instead. There was no room at the school, so the administration housed our class along with that of another teacher in an old building next to a pasture of grazing cattle. She chuckled as she talked about what it was like when the wind blew our way.

Despite the facilities our efforts were unimpeded. Typical of the supplies provided for Blacks in segregated public school systems of the Deep South, the books were tattered with markings indicating that officials of the school for whites had discarded them. I still recall my pointy finger dotting across stained pages of *The New Fun with Dick and Jane*, and hearing my parents and my teacher say, "Laurita, don't just call words. Read!" The 1954 decision in *Brown v. Board of Education* meant that Blacks in the county would eventually get a new school, a long brick building that housed grades 1- 12 with indoor plumbing and a cafeteria that served meals as required by what we referred to as the "school hot lunch program."

Administrative changes in the county school system prompted my parents to relocate to another rural Georgia county. There, I became even more aware of the racial divide. We settled in time for the October start of school. As late as the 1960s, many farmers still relied on manual labor to pick cotton and to harvest other crops. Therefore, county officials delayed the start of school until the bulk of the crops were in. In the town, the proverbial "other side of the track" was a reality. Blacks and whites crossed at the railroad track when walking to and from their respective schools. I do not recall any major racial incidents.

Seven years later our family now with four children, moved to South Florida where I completed my senior high school year. (Both of my parents were Floridians). I soon adjusted to the new school and applied to college at Tuskegee. The acceptance letter stated that I had been selected to participate in a freshmen experimental program, which involved an integrated curriculum of the social sciences taught by visiting professors. Included in the letter was a summer reading list. Among the books were *Mandingo* by Kyle Onstott, George Orwell's *1984*, and James Baldwin's *The Fire Next Time*. As though the list was not long enough my father added Booker T. Washington's *Up from Slavery*.

Early Exposure to Dietetics

Beyond what I learned at home about diet and health, my earliest impression of what I thought was dietetics was formed during my teens. While attending the General Conference of the African Methodist Episcopal Church in Louisville, Kentucky, the youth delegates were taken on a field trip to Dayton, Ohio where we toured the home of black poet Paul Laurence Dunbar, and to Wilberforce, Ohio to visit the campus of Wilberforce University. At the University, we ate in the campus dining hall. While waiting in line for meal service to begin, to my left I noticed a door behind the serving counter. When the door opened a woman emerged – a buxom woman dressed in a bright white uniform that was laundered to perfection!

Although she wore a hairnet, she was not like the lunch ladies of school cafeterias. The servers stepped back from the serving counter and waited while she carefully eyed each menu item and poked her thermometer to check the temperature of the hot foods. As she turned and strutted back toward her office door, she looked over her left shoulder and gave an authoritative nod of approval as if to say, "You may now begin." I did not know her job title, but her in-charge style impressed me.

I later learned that what the woman did at Wilberforce was akin to dietetics. That impression was so profound that I do not recall ever considering any career other than what I had come to believe was dietetics. Growing up during the late 1950s, my exposure to career choices was limited. Nearly all of the African American women college graduates I knew were public school teachers. During visits to black colleges or hospitals I saw African American women who were either professors or nurses. I recall seeing black Catholic nuns in Augusta, Georgia. I never considered entering the teaching or nursing profession, let alone a convent!

Although I was not sure about my choice, I began talking about becoming a dietitian. My dad thought differently. I do not think that his health had much to do with it, but he wanted me to study medicine. He would say, "If you are going to be on your feet all day working in a hospital, you might as well be a doctor." Being the obedient daughter that I was, and knowing about relatively few careers, in college I chose biology as a major, the typical choice for a pre-med student. After all, my parents were paying. However, I did not have the slightest intention of becoming a doctor! I still had food, diet and health in mind. Therefore, mid-way through my freshman year I changed to Food Administration, an undergraduate area of study that would prepare me for a post-baccalaureate internship in dietetics.

The focus of my undergraduate studies had been in Food Administration, but I later realized that I had no genuine interest in the administrative or managerial side of the dietetics profession, an area that entailed foodservice operations. My interest instead was in the impact of illness on nutritional needs. So I gravitated toward clinical dietetics which involves, but is not limited to the nutritional care of hospitalized patients. Fortunately, there was an opportunity for me to gain exposure to clinical dietetics beyond that offered in regular undergraduate college courses.

One of the requirements of my undergraduate curriculum was to complete a work-training experience during the summer following the junior year of college. A senior student advised me to go to Chicago. "Go to Michael Reese Hospital, she said." My parents were not sold on the idea of my going to a big city. I was only 19 years old, but since we had family there and since summer student interns lived in the nurse's residence on the hospital campus, they finally conceded and let me go. I dressed in my Sunday best as was the trend for air travel, and boarded an Eastern Airlines flight to O'Hare. I thought hard and long about how I could show my appreciation. It was decades later at my father's passing that I found the Father's Day card I had sent with the fifteen dollars still inside.

Hot Summer in the 60s

The "Windy City" had much to offer and I thought I had seen it all until one late August afternoon. While riding a Chicago Transit Authority bus I caught a view of what appeared to have been thousands of police and National Guardsmen. They were there to control the throng of Vietnam War protestors gathered outside the halls of the 1968 Democratic National Convention. I could hardly believe the tear gas smoke, wielding batons, and the resisting horizontal bodies that were being tossed into police vans, though they were typical of efforts to quell violent protests that marked the turbulent 1960s.

The scene was far greater than what I experienced back at Tuskegee when the murder of Sammy Younge, Jr. sparked days of unrest. Younge, who had worked with voter-registration and desegregating public facilities, was the first black student to die in the Civil Rights movement. A white service station attendant had murdered Sammy for attempting to use a "Whites Only" restroom at a Tuskegee gas station. The community and the campus were outraged. Two football players stormed the dormitory pounding on doors demanding that we come out and get involved. As we marched to downtown Tuskegee and sat for hours on a sidewalk that January afternoon all I could think was "What if my mama should see me on the evening news?" With all the newsworthy events in 1966, South Florida television was not likely to air coverage of protest in the little town of Tuskegee, Alabama, but that never crossed my mind. My mother's stern advice, "Don't go there and get yourself in trouble," now had an added interpretation: don't go there protesting and get kicked out of school.

I joined the march to downtown Tuskegee, but I refused to take part in the campus protest against the long-held tradition of compulsory chapel attendance. Attending Sunday worship activities had always been a part of my life. As did other students, I went to off-campus parties, rode in private cars without permission and broke curfew – college campus rules that are unheard of today. However, on Sunday morning I was at Sunday School, followed by Chapel and often-times Church service in the community. When military chaplains came to campus as guest speakers for Chapel or for other religious events, Tuskegee's Chaplain Andrew Johnson invited me to welcome and have dinner with them in the campus guesthouse. This was an honor. Therefore, even when Chapel attendance was no longer mandatory, I continued to go.

The summer at Michael Reese Hospital was memorable. The dietitians "took me under their wings" and made sure I received experience in both administrative and clinical dietetics. I am grateful that Mrs. Alma Gray, a Tuskegee alumna, patiently guided as I learned to calculate diets for patients with diabetes and for those with renal disease. I am thankful that dietitians, supervisors and staff allowed me to get the hands-on experience that taught me vital lessons about foodservice management and employee supervision which enhanced my appreciation of administrative dietetics.

After Chicago, I returned to Tuskegee to begin my senior college year. Among other courses, I still had another in foods. Part of the final examination for that course was the senior class project – a catered event. The theme, "Soul at Its Best," was timely in that the country was awakening to black culture. The assignment was to prepare for fifty guests. I opted to make the coffee. When the instructor, Mr. Jay B. King, saw me spooning coffee grounds into the large urn he asked, "Miss Mack, how many tablespoons are in a cup?" After a brief moment of panic, I recalled that using a disproportionately small measuring device is time-consuming and that inefficiency drives up labor cost. This was a principle of administrative dietetics; ignoring it almost lowered my grade for that class and ruined my grade point average.

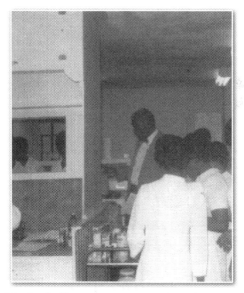

Mr. Jay B. King instructing students for senior
class project. Tuskegee Institute (Univ).

Still Discovering

I had reached my senior college year, but I was still unsure about dietetics. About midway through the year Mrs. Salona C. McDonald, Chief Dietitian, Internship Director and faculty member offered me the job of assisting her with her undergraduate teaching duties. Since I had helped my mother assemble teaching supplies, and make what were then mimeographed copies of handouts and exams the role of "teacher's helper" was familiar. Mrs. McDonald evidently recognized the ease with which I took on the responsibility and encouraged me to apply to a graduate program in nutrition. At her advice, along with my father's strong recommendation that I not seek employment without a master's degree, I applied for graduate school. I remained at Tuskegee for two more years and earned a Master of Science degree in Food Science and Human Nutrition. The Chicago undergraduate summer work-training experience and the practicum portion of college courses were as close as I came to doing a traditional post-baccalaureate hospital dietetic internship.

Graduate School

My research project for the master's degree thesis involved determining the effects of the artificial sweetener cyclamate on laboratory animals. We never received the mice we expected so my lab partner, Mary Reese Mickles, and I examined the effects of the sweetener on the internal organs of young chickens. After enduring the odor of warm sacrificed chicks, we thought we would never eat chicken again.

Mary Reese Mickles at Tuskegee Food Science Lab

Laurita at Tuskegee Food Science Lab

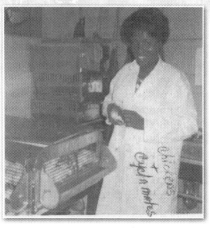

Food Science Lab with chicks for cyclamate research

EXPENSES AND FINANCIAL ASSISTANCE.

Internship. Full scholarship and entire maintenance are provided. The application fee ($10.00) is paid by the intern, and also medical fees each term, $20.00 per semester and $10.00 in the summer. Uniforms and shoes are furnished by the intern. Transportation to Birmingham, Alabama to take the examination for registration is an individual expense.

Graduate Study. Tuition is presently $500 per semester and $250 for the summer term. Room and Board is $362.50 per semester and $225 for summer. A limited number of graduate assistantships and Public Health Traineeships are available, starting at $3,000. (All fees are subject to change.)

Tuskegee Institute (Univ.) brochure.
Dr. Ronald A. Chung (left) observing
graduate food science majors

When it was time for the oral exam Dr. Ronald Chung my major professor was there to assure me that I was ready. He nodded proudly as Dr. Johnnie Prothro, a nutritional biochemist drilled me on one of her favorite topics - nitrogen balance. Anyone who ever took a class from her knows that it was the way she asked questions rather than what she asked. I passed the oral exam and in April was on my way to Miami, Florida to interview for a position with the Dade County Department of Public Health.

Beginning of a Career

After working several months in Maternal and Infant Care, I became head of Miami's newly-funded Model Cities Nutrition Project. Also working in public health was the man I would later marry. My immediate supervisor was a member of the American Dietetic Association (now the Academy of Nutrition and Dietetics). With a master's degree, I could work under her supervision for one year and then be eligible to sit for the registration examination, which if passed, would grant the credential of registered dietitian (RD). I passed the RD exam, but working in community nutrition, my title was public health nutritionist rather than registered dietitian. Since that time, the Academy of Nutrition and Dietetics has adopted the title registered dietitian nutritionist, thus the current designation RDN.

Through employment with the federally funded Model Cities and a hospital-based Supplemental Nutrition Program for Women Infants and Children(WIC), I gained experience in supervising community outreach workers, office staff, and in providing direct nutrition care to clients in out- and in-patient settings.

Model Cities Clinic, Nutrition Office, Miami, FL

Although I began in community public health nutrition, and later spent the greater portion of my career in higher education helping to prepare students for careers in dietetics, nursing and medicine, I had some clinical experience along the way. My husband's work as a public health advisor transferred us from Miami to Chicago, and after nearly two years of being a housewife and mother, I began work as a registered dietitian in a suburban hospital.

I recall an event that took me back to my initial interest in dietetics. One morning I arrived just as the chief clinical dietitian was reviewing a stack of menus on which patients had circled their selections for the following day. She was doing a double check, as I had already looked through them the evening before. Removing the menu of an elderly heart patient who had died during the night, she noticed that I had failed to cross out scrambled egg and write in "egg substitute." Embarrassed, I apologized as she lightly chided me about the error. When the chief left the office, the diet technician who had overheard the conversation, sympathetically whispered, "Don't worry Mrs. Burley, he told me several times in Italian how much he wanted a real egg." I thanked the diet technician for her efforts to assuage my embarrassment and guilt, but I had mixed emotions.

On one hand, I thought that if he longed for a real egg up to the very end of his life, I probably had not made that error before and, therefore, did not cause his demise. On the other hand, I thought, it would have been a pleasure to grant a dying man such a simple wish, a breakfast with scrambled egg fresh from the shell! The whole gaffe begged the question, "In cardiovascular disease, just how much harm could one egg cause?" Over the years, there have been numerous studies about the effect of eggs and other foods on blood cholesterol levels and heart disease. Despite my interest, I have had relatively little experience as a clinical nutrition researcher.

LAURITA M. BURLEY, PH.D. RDN, LD

Perhaps had there been a Professional Development Portfolio as the Academy of Nutrition and Dietetics now requires of its members, I would have given more thought to the direction my career was taking.

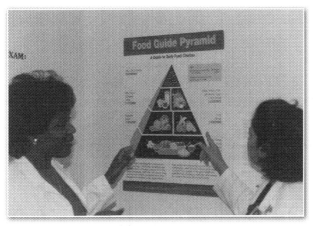

Reviewing Food Guide Pyramid with Dr. R. Singh,
Family Medicine resident physician. Atlanta, GA.

Fulfilling a Dream

When it came to employment, shaping my career path was not a top priority. My husband's work took us to different states and as a black wife and mother, I did not fully relate to the movement for women's liberation of the 1970s. So when it was time to move, I followed. We did not live any place very long before I found employment. I accepted positions in clinical dietetics and in academia. It was the academic environment that reminded me of something I said one summer while helping my mother decorate the bulletin board in her classroom. An onlooker, a male teacher asked about my plans for the future, and then called out, "Did you hear that Mrs. Mack? She said that one day she's going to be 'Dr. somebody.'" With an emphasis on somebody, rather than on

Dr., he seemed to have been more interested in seeing how my mother would react. Nevertheless, I became Mrs. Burley first, and 32 years later, Dr. Burley.

Pursuing doctoral studies was not a straightforward process. Once again, I found myself having to make a career choice. To get back into student mode, I began auditing classes before I actually enrolled in a doctoral program: first, in a master's level nutrition course and later in a biochemistry class with medical students. Now living in Atlanta, Georgia and not wanting to commute to The University of Georgia in Athens, I completed two courses in Atlanta at Georgia State University (GSU) toward a doctoral degree in Human Resources, one in adult education and the other in statistics. I later learned that GSU offered a doctorate in Educational Policy Studies, with a concentration in higher education.

That's it! I thought. The first course, History of Higher Education, was interesting but I soon found myself pondering whether to remain at GSU and learn more about the history of Haa vad (Harvard) or return to the Morehouse School of Medicine and continue the refresher in biochemistry with cellular processes, carbon chains and carboxyl groups! I remained at GSU and eventually came to enjoy Educational Policy Studies. With a focus on sociohistorical and cultural analysis and with the patient support of my Committee Chair, Philo Hutcherson, I wrote a dissertation on the meaning of profession, and for a case study examined the history of the dietetics program at Tuskegee Institute (now Tuskegee University).

Graduation day with Philo Hutcheson, Committee Chair and
Dissertation Director, Georgia State University, Atlanta, GA

When asked why I waited or what took so long for me to return
to school, I have but one answer – "Life!" Looking back, I seldom
missed Sunday School, teacher conferences, family mealtimes,
date nights, fishing trips and opportunities to drive my children to
Girl- or Boy Scout meetings, to camp, or to sit through baseball,
softball, football and soccer practices and games. Life did not stop
after I entered the doctoral program. In addition to my regular job
responsibilities, along the way I agreed to a guest faculty position and
taught a course for one semester, volunteered as a program reviewer
for what was then the Commission on Accreditation for Dietetics
Education. Completing the doctoral program took a while, but I
enjoyed the journey. My only regret is that my parents, my husband
and some of the women I interviewed for the dissertation research
did not live to see me receive the diploma. Fortunately, my two
children-- one in and the other just out of graduate school, along
with my daughter-in-law, twin grandsons (then four months old),
my sisters, an uncle, and other family members and friends were at
the graduation ceremony to help celebrate.

Graduation day with family members, Georgia State University, Atlanta, GA. L-R: Heather (daughter-in-law) with Victor (grandson); Tanesha (daughter); William (son) with Vincent (grandson).

Experience as an African American in Dietetics

Beyond the story of how I arrived at where I am today, there is the question of my experience as an African American employed in a predominantly white profession. Early on, life afforded me opportunities that involved relating to other races. Despite having grown up during segregation, my parents, teachers and college professors made it possible for me to engage in activities outside of the black community. For example, in college we attended meetings at or participated in student exchange programs with the University of Kentucky, Georgia and Alabama, which during the 1960s and early 1970s were predominantly white universities.

Overall, I have not had any unusual experiences because of my race, but some occurrences were less subtle than others were. I recall applying to a county school system for the position of registered dietitian. Despite my having the credentials, MS, RD, the white male interviewer said, "Most of our girls start out in the kitchen and work their way up to supervisor." I was not sure whether he had a pre-conceived notion that all African Americans applying for employment in foodservice needed to start with the basics regardless of education and experience or if he had someone else in mind for the job. I simply thanked him for his time, asked for my resume and left.

There have been other occasions involving race. I have had white higher-ups or colleagues discredit my input or credit my contributions to another individual of their race. One hospital occurrence was clearly a matter of racial bias. While working in Illinois, I responded to a complaint from a disgruntled white patient who was so upset about her food that she demanded to see a dietitian. When I walked into her hospital room, she shouted, "I didn't send for a girl from the kitchen. I asked to see the dietitian!" Although I was wearing a white uniform bearing the professional emblem of the American Dietetic Association, and was carrying the metal card tray used by dietitians to record notes on each patient, I obviously did not meet her image of a dietitian. I remained at her bedside until she calmed down, and with the same air of the woman I had seen at Wilberforce, I promised the patient that upon my return to the dietitians' office, I would register her complaint with the kitchen staff.

The above occurrences were not uncommon during the 1970s, and the positives of my career have far outweighed any racial discrimination I actually encountered or imagined. In several positions, I have been the first or the only registered dietitian nutritionist, an employment condition that afforded a lot of creativity and independence in managing and coordinating programs. My work with the Miami Model Cities Project, for example, involved hiring and supervising nutrition outreach workers, selecting equipment and material, and coordinating programs with other public health team members to provide nutrition education services to the Model Cities community.

As a teacher, I have developed or adapted nutrition curricula for didactic and clinical training of students in medicine, nursing and for those in social work as well as for students in dietetics and nutrition. It is always a pleasure to hear a student recall something useful that they learned. I too, thank the many teachers, the community and my family members for helping to shape my career path, and for life lessons I learned along the way.

Finally, the nutrition and dietetics profession attracts many "experts," both trained and untrained. The range of work settings is broad, and the profession offers a myriad of opportunities. I encourage dietitians entering the field that when opportunities present, get involved in the decision-making that affects their work, and to participate locally and nationally in organizations of the nutrition and dietetics profession. I further encourage them to stay positive, and to keep up-to-date with advancements in the profession, especially in their area of expertise. Nutrition and dietetics is an exciting field! I advise beginners to set goals, but without over-restricting the scope, and to identify a mentor early in their career.

KEEP YOUR EYES ON THE ROAD

Annie B. Carr

*P*op-Pa, my paternal grandfather always had a large vegetable garden. That garden fed our family and half of the neighborhood. I'd watch Pop-Pa till the rows of dirt, drop seeds in the ground and water that garden. I couldn't wait for the plants to burst thru – mustard greens, tomatoes, cucumbers, corn, green beans, peas, cabbage, cauliflower, and broccoli. You name it; he grew it. Pop-Pa even grew a special type of corn that we popped for our family. Yes, as a child I didn't know that garden was the beginning of an education that would sustain me for the rest of my life.

Pop-pa, Titus Carr, was a widower and it was with the profits from his garden that he contributed to the education of his three daughters, two of whom earned a college degree.

My father, Henry Carr, Sr. added to the vegetable garden, with fruit trees in our yard: pears, peaches, figs, lemons, and kumquat. My mother, Annie Mae Pratt Carr, cooked and canned the fruits and vegetables for the winter months. My duties were to clean and prepare the fruits and vegetables for canning. I got so sick and tired of peeling, slicing, snapping, shelling and shucking! My father gave my sister, brother and me the opportunity to sell some of the vegetables from his garden. He felt it was a way to teach us to weigh, count, and to interact with people. It also taught us "buying power" and how to save to purchase those items our little hearts desired.

Daddy and Mom-ma worked very hard to provide opportunities for us to grow inside and outside of our small community of Patterson, Louisiana. Yet, I must admit that my brother, Henry and I were not happy about selling vegetables, but my older sister, Phyllis enjoyed the job. She would carry bagged vegetables on her bicycle throughout the neighborhood. Being older, she understood the value of having her own money.

I did not like selling the products from our family's garden but I certainly enjoyed our family meals. In addition to our vegetable garden, our menus included fresh shrimp, fish, and crabs -- staple items on the menus due to family members or friends working at the docks in Patterson and Berwick. Another family member worked at the meat market in Patterson, so we had fresh cuts of meats too. Sometimes we even raised the meat that we ate.

I clearly remember all the trips with the family to visit Daddy's aunt in Port Barre, Louisiana and returning home with piglets in the trunk of our car. The task of caring for and feeding the piglets until slaughter time was given to my brother and me. Again, this was my father's way of teaching us responsibility. Daddy always said, "Hard work pays off in the end." I must admit, I could not eat the pork meat; I think my fat cells started to develop from eating butter and rice instead of pork roast, chops, and loins from our family pet. Maybe, I am just a rice eating Geechee!

Lessons for Life

It seems that in so many ways, food has always been more than just substance in our family, but little did I know how much a part of my life it would eventually become. Nearly everything that I learned as I grew up helped contribute to what and who I am today.

Auntie, my mother's baby sister, Mary Jane Pratt Rhodes was employed in food services by Calcasieu Parish Public Schools for 42 years. She became the lead baker for a high school and excelled in making yeast rolls, cinnamon rolls, melt-in-your-mouth pie crusts, pecan tarts, and pound cakes. It was from Auntie that I learned the skill of baking. Every Sunday I was the one who made bakery products for the family and dinner guests. However, it was Mom- ma who taught me the essentials of Southern cooking. I learned to make fudge, pralines, rice, red beans, roux (gravy), and of course the best cornbread, the kind made in a seasoned cast iron skillet. The recipes below are some of my family favorites that I know you will enjoy!

Louisiana Red Beans

1 lb. Camellia Red Kidney Beans
½ lb. seasoning meat or ham (optional for vegetarian diet)
8-10 cups of water
1 medium onion, chopped
2 cloves garlic, chopped
3 tbs. celery, chopped
3 tbs. parsley, chopped
2 large bay leaves
Salt and pepper to taste or may use Tony Chachere's Original Creole Seasoning

Rinse and sort beans. In a large pot, add beans with 3-4 cups of water to soak, soak beans overnight. Pour off soaking water, add 8-10 cups of water. Bring to a boil for 15 minutes.

In a separate skillet, brown meat and set aside, reserving fat drippings. In drippings, sauté chopped vegetables (onion, celery, garlic, and parley). Add meat, vegetables, and bay leaves to beans. Add salt, pepper, and Cajun seasonings (optional) to taste. Reduce heat, cover, and simmer stirring occasionally, for about 1 to 1 ½ hours, or until tender. For creamier consistency, when beans are soft, crush some of the beans against the side of the pot with a large spoon. Add water while cooking if necessary. Serves 6-8. Serve beans over cooked rice.

Nutrients per 1 cup/Serving
Calories (kcal) 122.5
Fat (g) 2.5
Cholesterol (mg) 16.2
Sodium (mg) 279.2
Potassium (mg) 353.4
Carbohydrate (g) 13.9
Fiber (g) 3.9
Protein (g) 11.3

Auntie's Pecan Pies

Two 12, or one 24 1-inch muffin pan, greased with butter
Crust:
One 3 oz. package cream cheese
½ cup butter
1 cup + 1 tablespoon sifted all-purpose flour

Combine in mixing bowl cream cheese, butter, and flour until well blended dough. Break pieces of dough and press with fingers into each greased muffin pan, making sure to cover the sides of the muffin pan.

Filling:
1 whole egg, beaten
½ cup dark brown sugar, firmly packed
¼ cup granulated sugar
1 tablespoon melted butter
1 teaspoon pure vanilla
¾ cup pecans, chopped
1/8 teaspoon salt

Combine all ingredients into a mixing bowl and stir until well blended. Spoon filling into 1 inch muffin pan, filling to the top. Bake in 350 degree oven for 25 minutes or until golden brown. Cool for 5 minutes. Remove from muffin pan with a pointed knife being careful not to break the crust. Store in a tightly sealed container to keep fresh. Make 24 individual pies.

These pies are great any time of the year but our family always had Auntie's Pecan Pies at the Christmas Holidays. Auntie started to make her own delicious pie crust after a year of using the above crust recipe.

Nutrients per Serving
Calories (kcal) 124.7
Fat (g) 8.5
Saturated Fat (g) 3.8
Cholesterol (mg) 23.9
Sodium (mg) 59.1
Potassium (mg) 34.5
Carbohydrate (g) 11.2
Sugar (g) 6.8

My parents were a daily example of strong "faith." I can't remember a time when they weren't working more than one job to provide for us. We were taught that on Sunday you attend church or Sunday school first. You could engage in other activities later.

Others in our small community were also examples of how to live one's life. When I was growing up, Blacks attended Hattie A. Watts Elementary and High School, which was named for the first Black teacher in Patterson. The teachers were excellent mentors, dedicated to helping us not only with school work, but with our community, our families and our personal growth and development. They were all excellent mentors.

My high school home economics teacher also taught me to cook and to sew. I was better at sewing than cooking. I did, however win the home economics award at my high school. Nevertheless, I didn't consider home economics as a major in college because I would have to teach, and I didn't want to teach. But I knew without a doubt that I was going to college.

Phyllis, my sister nine years my senior was in college when I was in the fourth grade. My father's two sisters, Emma Dell Carr and Evelyn Carr were college educated and they were teachers. All of the college educated, African American females in my hometown were teachers. So, since mathematics was my best subject in high school, I made the decision as a senior that I would explore the area of accounting as a major. I did not want to be an educator in the classroom. Yet, I did learn about the field of Dietetics in my junior/senior years at Hattie A. Watts High School.

My high school government teacher's wife, Ann Williams was a Dietitian. She attended Southern University in Baton Rouge, LA and was completing a Dietetic Internship when I met her. Although she would come to Patterson to visit some weekends, I don't remember asking her any questions about the field of Dietetics. My career choice was to become an accountant.

It was during my freshmen year at Southern University that I changed my mind about that.

Annie Carr, Freshman at Southern University in
Baton Rouge, LA, in the Triangle Complex

I asked one of the dorm matrons about majoring in accounting and she informed me that I would have to stay up all night studying. That was enough to make me decide that accounting wasn't for me. I had to rethink my major. It was then that I started thinking about the Dietitian, Ann Williams and decided to seek more information. My sophomore year I enrolled in the Food and Nutrition Program in the College of Home Economics. Being young and immature, we sometimes make life decision based on someone's comments without researching the course requirements. The course requirements for the Foods and Nutrition program were mainly the sciences and included a combination of lecture and lab for a total seven hours per week for 4 hours of credit per semester. As an example, the accounting classes were three hours per week for 3 hours credit per semester. Smart me, I still had to study all night with the sciences.

My three years in the Department of Foods and Nutrition were very exciting and fulfilling with new classmates and friends. I had good instructors and I learned a lot, more than food service. Mrs. Verda Pass taught all the Personnel and Food Management, Layout and Design courses in the Department. Mrs. Pass was structured, articulate and persistent and expected the best from her students. She would walk into the classroom at 8:00 a.m. and say, "Good morning class!" and no one would answer. She'd repeat herself and say "Good morning class," explaining to us that we should always speak to employees because staff doesn't need to know if you are having a good or bad day. To this day, that principle is a part of my everyday home and work environment.

Annie Carr in Experimental Food Lab

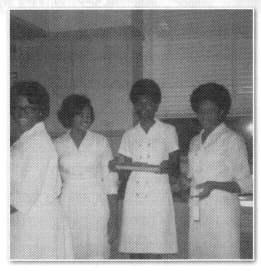

Annie Carr with classmates in Experimental Food Lab

Just as there had been in Patterson, there were instructors at Southern University who cared about students and were dedicated/committed in getting students through the program.

The required Home Management course at Southern was taught by Mrs. Hunter and the course was divided into two segments. The first part was the classroom lecture and the second part was the practicum in which we lived in the house for six weeks. For one week we each had assigned duties. I was the first cook in my group and I decided to bake a duck for our Thanksgiving meal. Well, this was my first time cooking a duck and I over cooked the bird. Mrs. Hunter was very critical and said, "Carr, you cooked the duck until all the meat is falling off the bone." I haven't cooked a duck since that experience in the home management house.

Mrs. Hunter was meticulous when it came to educating her students. The students living in the house would eat three meals together. We had a house curfew of 11:00 p.m. She would actually use white gloves to check our daily dusting of the furniture. Now, the things we did to maintain the house by Mrs. Hunter's standards may seem funny today, but it didn't feel that way at the time. Living in the home management house at the time I was pledging Delta Sigma Theta Sorority, Inc., Alpha Tau Chapter was a time-management challenge. Yet, I prevailed.

Standing in front of the Home Management House

Ms. Pinkie Thrift, Dean of the College of Home Economics was extremely direct with me in the selection of my dietetic internships. My criteria for an internship were that it be someplace close to home or near a relative. She, however totally ignored my two program choices. Instead, Ms. Thrift informed me that I should apply to two other programs. In April, I was offered a 12 month program at Cleveland Hospital and a six month program at Indiana University Medical Center. I selected Indiana University Medical Center in Indianapolis for a six month Dietetic Internship with graduate courses included to start in October of the same year. My graduation from Southern University and A&M College with a B.S. degree in Foods and Nutrition came in May.

Annie Carr and Connie Clark (deceased) on Graduation Day

Over the summer, I landed a job in New Orleans with the Louisiana Cooperative Extension as a Nutrition Aide. In this position I instructed families on how to use USDA Food Commodities in their everyday food preparation. For example: making a "Master Mix" using commodity flour that could be used to make biscuits, pancakes and breads. I worked there for three months before moving, not only from the South but far from my family, friends and those who nurtured me. My adventure in life to become a Registered Dietitian had begun.

Internship Experiences

On October 1, 1970 I arrived in Indianapolis, IN to enter my Dietetic Internship Program. This was my first time being so far from home. I was excited and didn't know what to expect. But inside I was sad that I was such a long way from family and friends. I did not know anyone in Indianapolis, IN. I knew that this was my first and big step to being an adult with only me to depend on for what happened in a program that would determine my future in dietetics.

When I arrived at the dormitory on campus, my roommate, Linda Grissom was already in the room. Linda was married and like me she would be apart from loved ones during her internship. She and her husband would be separated for the next six months. One other thing we had in common was that for the first time in our lives we would be interacting with a person of a different race on a more personal level. You see, Linda was Caucasian. It appeared that she knew about me sharing a room with her prior to my arrival and had no objection. I never asked, but I believed my internship director had shared with Linda that we would be roommates. Linda and I respected each other and were very good roommates.

In the dorm room next to ours lived Juanita Huff, an African American, who was a social worker earning a Master's degree. She was completing her experience at La Rue Carter Hospital, which was a part of the Indiana University Medical Center complex. Not only did Juanita have a car which provided us with the opportunity to get away from campus and explore the city, but she introduced me to other African American women on campus. These relationships served to offer me a sense of normalcy during the stressful six month period of my internship. Up to this day, Juanita Huff, now Mrs. Juanita Huff Wilson remains my dear friend.

In a lot of ways, Indianapolis proved to be a very educational experience for me. I arrived in the city with my best leather coat, lined in nylon. I almost froze in that coat! Who knew that the winters in the Midwest could get that cold?

In addition to my weather discoveries, I also discovered that out of six interns in my program, I was the only Black. The only other

African Americans anywhere near the program were the cooks and their supervisor, the clerks and the porters on the floors. The workers in the kitchen were very helpful and friendly to me, always offering me food to eat.

The dietitians on staff at the I.U. Medical Center were not the friendly type. They never invited the interns out for any type of social outings, but I do remember that our department secretary invited us over one evening during the Christmas holidays. The Christmas of 1970 was my first time being away from my family for that special holiday, and like the other interns I had to work on Christmas Day. Not being with my family made me realize the importance of us being together for the holidays. That had been so important to me for the last 22 years of my life. I felt a void not being at home. I made a call to Mom-ma and Daddy to wish them a Merry Christmas and as usual all the family members were at my parents for Christmas. I felt alone and sad not to be home with everyone. After that year, I made a commitment to myself that I would be home for every Christmas after that.

As my internship progressed, I learned a lot about the other interns in my dietetic program. I learned the ways in which we were similar and the ways we were different as well. One of the things I began to realize was how limited my world had been. Some of my fellow interns talked about their travels to European countries and other places around the world. They would gush about how much they enjoyed traveling. At the time, I could only listen because I had nothing to add to these conversations. Prior to traveling to Indiana, I had only been on family vacations to cities in Texas (Galveston Beach & Six Flags over Texas in Arlington) and in Louisiana (Pontchartrain Beach), but that was about to change. I made another commitment that I would see the World.

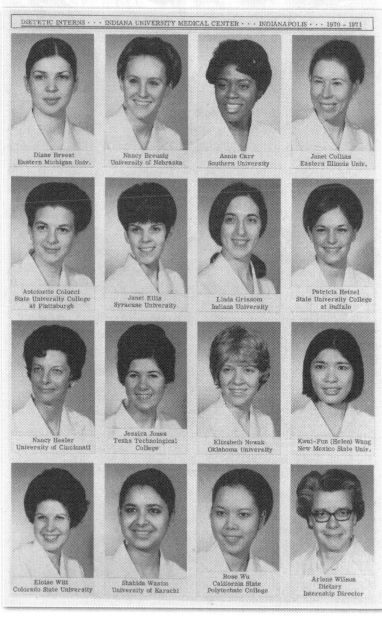

DIETETIC INTERNS · · · INDIANA UNIVERSITY MEDICAL CENTER · · · INDIANAPOLIS · · · 1970 - 1971

Diane Breest
Eastern Michigan Univ.

Nancy Breunig
University of Nebraska

Annie Carr
Southern University

Janet Collins
Eastern Illinois Univ.

Antoinette Colucci
State University College
at Plattsburgh

Janet Ellis
Syracuse University

Linda Grissom
Indiana University

Patricia Hetzel
State University College
at Buffalo

Nancy Hesler
University of Cincinnati

Jessica Jones
Texas Technological
College

Elizabeth Nowak
Oklahoma University

Kwai-Fun (Helen) Wang
New Mexico State Univ.

Eloise Witt
Colorado State University

Shahida Wasim
University of Karachi

Rose Wu
California State
Polytechnic College

Arlene Wilson
Dietary
Internship Director

Dietetic Internship Class- Indiana University
Medical Center, Indianapolis, IN

ANNIE B. CARR, MS, RDN

The work as a dietetic intern at the Indiana University Medical Center could be grueling. I worked a regular split shift staring at 6:00 am usually off 1-4 pm and ending at 6:00 pm, covering three meals on the floors. We were always short of workers on the weekends and this would be the time that the interns were in charge. When staff didn't come to work on the floors of the hospital, we had to cover taking trays to, and collecting them from patients, plus loading and unloading the dishwashing machine.

One experience that I would like to share is my rotation on the 5th floor of the hospital. This floor was reserved for dignitaries in the hospital and the services were with silver, crystal, and china. A patient requested a bottle of Mateus wine from the menu. The hospital had the bottle of wine, but I couldn't find a wine bottle opener. So, what should one do in this situation? I used a knife to get the cork out of the bottle. Pieces of the cork fell into the wine. I was successful in taking the cork out but had to strain the wine and pour the wine back into the bottle. This situation also required an explanation to the patient because it appeared to have taken a long time for me to get through the process. In the end, it worked out but the stress to make it happen was tremendous.

Our graduate classes were taught twice a week for two hours. We worked just about every weekend for the duration of the internship. As my internship ended, I did have one weekend to remember.

On that rare weekend off, Juanita Huff and I took a road trip to Chicago to visit her sister. It was my first trip to the Windy City. It was exciting seeing all the sights that I had read about. This was the best weekend I had during the entire internship.

During my internship, I met three fellow Southern University graduates in the city who were also fellow Registered Dietitians. We met at the Central District Dietetic Association meetings. Their names were Jerrie Player, Ina Jackson and Eva Board. Over the years they and other African American dietitians were very helpful in assisting me with making the adjustment in Indianapolis and in my career.

Life after an Internship

As a full-time graduate student with a limited stipend, I was offered a job at Indiana University Medical Center cafeteria on the weekends as the cashier and manager to help support myself. I would also tally the production worksheets for the next day's meals for the cooks. I realized that my part time job was robbing me of my weekends to study, attend church and limiting my social life. I really needed a job to pay rent and utilities because my stipend was just not enough to pay the bills.

I attended Indianapolis University-Purdue University at Indianapolis (IUPUI) campus for most of my classes; however, some of my classes were at Butler University. Life was not easy going to night classes until 9:00 pm without transportation. I remember taking public transportation or walking to IUPUI campus and at Butler University asking classmates to drop me off at the nearest bus stop. Without a car at the time, I did the best that I could.

Reaching Back to Help Someone

My saving grace was Theresa McDuffie Samuels, an African American Registered Dietitian/Nutritionist in Indianapolis, IN, who befriended me during my Dietetic Internship. She was Chief Public Health Nutritionist for Marion County Health Department. Theresa heard my cry of working on the weekends and hired me part-time to work for the Marion County Health Department as a Nutritionist for the Well Baby Clinics. The location of the clinic was walking distance from my apartment and I worked part-time on regular week days with my evening classes. Oh yes, no more weekends. When I completed my Master's Degree she hired me full-time. Theresa exposed me to many people including Dr. Frank Johnson, Director of the Marion County Health Department, and others in the profession by inviting me to luncheon meetings with nutritionists from other state agencies. She encouraged me to become involved with the Central District Dietetic Association. That spurred me to serve on local committees and eventually to serve as Chair of the Nominating Committee and this provided opportunities for qualified African American Registered Dietitians to be on the ballot and become elected officers in the District. The Central District Dietetic Association had six African American Registered Dietitians. I served as the treasurer and later the President-elect and the President of the Central District Dietetic Association. As President of the District Association, I served on the Indiana Dietetic Association as a district representative, later becoming the State Treasurer of the Association.

National Nutrition Month- Mary Carter, President of Indiana Dietetic Association; Bill Hudnut, Mayor; Annie Carr, President of Central District Dietetic Association; top row: left to right, Theresa Samuels (deceased), (unknown name), Colette Zyrkowski, and Jerrie Player.

Writing Checks as Treasurer of the Indiana Dietetic Association

My good fortune as a Registered Dietitian continued when Jerrie Player, a fellow Southern University graduate hired me as a Nutritionist and as her assistant for the Maternal and Infant Project (M & I) in January of 1972. Yet without a car, Jerrie was kind enough to pick me up every day for work. Several months into the job, she had to take a medical leave and I needed to purchase a car and bought a blue Camaro from one of my old dorm mates. But unfortunately I had one little problem. I didn't have a driver's license and no real driving experience!

Indiana's law required a 60 day wait before getting a license, but I couldn't wait that long. I had to get to work. So, the daring young Registered Dietitian who hadn't traveled very much, and was in need of some driving and parking practice to say the least, decided at the last minute to fly to Patterson, LA and take the written and driving test. That way I could get my license in one day. My thought was that I could drive just like anyone. June, my brother (Henry Carr, Jr.) stated, "If you keep your eyes on the road, you'll be okay. Guess what? I passed the test, received my driver license, and was on my way back to Indianapolis the next day.

The Maternal and Infant Care Project was valuable in helping me develop a wide range of skills when it came to working in a clinic environment -- developing materials, consulting, supervising, team work, and making home visits. In the clinic, we depended on nurses, social workers, nutritionists and community workers in order to provide the best care to our clients. I came out of that work experience not only with a plethora of knowledge but with two great friends, Crystal Rhodes and Jacquelyn Green. At the time both were social workers for the M & I Program. Eventually, Crystal became a successful author and playwright and Jackie went on to earn her PhD in Social Work, becoming, not only an author but an esteemed lecturer both in the United States and aboard.

Ina Jackson, a fellow Registered Dietitian and Southern University graduate and I formed a business as consultants to nursing homes in Indianapolis and the surrounding areas. Before going to our regular 8-4:30 jobs, we started our days with food service reviews at 6:00 a.m. to observe the breakfast preparation. We also did our consultant business on Saturdays and a few Sundays out of the year. We surely enjoyed those Saturday work days. We'd work for four hours and on our way home from an appointment we would stop and shop, spending just about all of the money we had made that day!

Ina Jackson (deceased) and Annie Carr attending the
American Dietetic Association in Philadelphia, PA

My next work experience was rewarding and at the same time extremely frustrating. I was hired as the Child Care and Summer Food Service Administrator at the Department of Public Instruction. This job was community based, and I worked with community organizations on the implementation of the USDA programs. The Federal Regulations were already determined and the challenge was training staff in the field who were political appointees without formal education. As Federal funding was made available for the first time by USDA for Nutrition Education, I was asked to become a Nutrition Educator for the state. This work involved developing nutrition education materials for schools and child care centers. I monitored the grants with the universities on the development of various nutrition education tools.

Teaching Nutrition to Educators in Gary, IN

It was expected that all employees of the department contribute to the campaign of the elected officials. I chose not to contribute to the campaign knowing that I would not progress in that environment. In 1985, Gwen Rossell, MS, RD, Maternal and Child Director at the Indiana Department of Health approached me about working for the agency. Without an interview, I was hired as a Nutrition Consultant. As a Consultant, I would be working with local health departments, school-based clinics and other agencies on maternal and infant care issues. Our phenomenal team consisted of Kathy Weaver, RN., MPH and Charles Brandenburg, M.S.W. and we covered the northern portion of the state. As a team, we worked very well together in the best interest of public health. Finally, I could see again how team decisions made a difference in the operation of state programs.

State Board of Health, Maternal and Child Health Division Team, Annie Carr, Nancy Simon, Chuck Brandenburg, and Kathy Weaver.

American Public Health Association Poster Session-Sharon Farris, Maureen McLean, Michelle Davis and Annie Carr

It was during these five years that my friendships were sealed with two Registered Dietitians from Gary, Indiana. These two Registered Dietitians were Tuskegee Institute graduates who were my friends and very supportive of me in my role as a Consultant with the State Board of Health and an elective officer of the Dietetic Association. During my overnight trips traveling to Gary, I would stay in their homes instead of staying in the local hotels. They were my supporters professionally and personally.

I had the opportunity to work with Collette Zyrkowski, MPH who was assigned to work in the Midwest Regional Office of HHS and later in Indianapolis in the Public Health Corp. It was she who shared with me information about a nutritionist position that would be opening at the Centers for Disease Control. I waited over a year to hear more about this new position. Meanwhile, in 1989, the doors of opportunities and recognitions opened for me.

It started in April with being the recipient of the Indianapolis Star Jefferson Award for Distinguished Public Service. This award was based on my community work as the founder of Black College Tour sponsored by Chi Chapter of Delta Sigma Theta Sorority, Inc. This project provided African American students in the city of Indianapolis an opportunity to visit several Historically Black College and Universities during spring break for a nominal fee. This premier project has existed for more than thirty years in the Indianapolis community. As of spring break 2015, I greeted more than 40 students visiting the Atlanta area Historically Black Colleges and Universities.

The second part of the Jefferson Award recognition was for being the Chairperson of the Indianapolis 100 Black Women fund-raising event for Homes for Black Children, Infant Mortality Project. This project addresses the lives of Black babies in the community and at the time, Indianapolis had one of the highest infant mortality rates in the country.

On July 9, 1988 at the 75th National Convention of Delta Sigma Theta Sorority, Inc. in Los Angeles, CA I was selected as one of the 75 Deltas recognized for outstanding public service in the Sorority. The event was such a lovely evening to remember with my Sorors from Indianapolis. This award was based on being the founder of the Black College Tour and coordinating the tour without a budget from the Sorority, and in the first year of the project taking two buses with over 80 students.

The State Board of Health under the leadership of Dr. Woodrow Myers surprised me with a front page special issue of The Indiana State Board of Health Newsletter. The Newsletter featured me as the winner of the Jefferson Award and included an interview with me talking about my work in the community.

When Will I Hear from CDC?

Finally, around the first of May I received a telephone call from CDC. It was Faye Wong, MPH, RD, Team Leader, and Nutrition Surveillance Branch informing me that I made the certification and was selected for an interview. My experiences with the employee's application process in Indianapolis were simple when compared to the preparation required for a federal job. The long form applicants must complete requires detailed and complete answers. Applications are scored and rated. I scored 100% for the certification and was selected for an interview.

By the middle of May, I was invited to Atlanta for an interview. The interview process consisted of giving a presentation and providing a scrap book of my work experiences and community involvement. My interview was with six Division leads and there were over 30 people in the audience to hear my presentation based on my work at the State Board of Health as well as previous public health experiences. June 1, 1989 I was notified that I was selected for the position out of 40 candidates who applied.

CDC – Here I Come

I began my journey with the CDC on July 3, 1989 as a Public Health Nutritionist working with states on the Pediatric Nutrition Surveillance Program. Three positions had been created for the newly formed National Center for Chronic Disease Prevention and Health Promotion, and mine was one of them.

For about four years, we the Pediatric and Prenatal Surveillance Team (Faye Wong, Colette Zyrkowski, Sarah Kuester, and Abe Pranvata, including our secretarial support Wanda Price and Charlotte Ross) worked on Nutrition Surveillance Programs, monitoring the state programs progress, producing reports, developing presentations, and making site visits to the state programs. We had the opportunity to work with the state nutritionists who worked mainly in Maternal and Child Health. Some people, however were working on the 5-A-Day Program. Our Division developed a strong relationship with American Cancer Society as we promoted the 5-A-Day programs and materials development.

American Public Health Association Poster Display-
CDC Annie Carr and Faye Wong.

Our National Center for Chronic Disease Prevention and Health Promotion started the sponsorship of an annual Chronic Disease Directors Conference. As part of the Center, we, the Nutritionists attended the first conference in San Diego, CA. CDC nutritionists were focused on developing and growing Chronic Disease Nutritionists in the states. I was charged with coordinating the first Chronic Disease Nutritionist meeting. We worked very hard to provide the training on best practices and the sharing of various state programs.

Chronic Disease Nutrition Conference- Coordinator
of the Nutrition Conference

Chronic Disease Nutrition Training Conference –Nutrition is Prevention
(Faye Wong, Annie Carr, Judy Foreso, and Colette Zyrkowski)

Coordinator of Chronic Disease Nutrition Reception

After several years of bringing the nutritionists together, we were faced with budget cutbacks. The Branch Chief asked me to think and be creative in providing training to state nutritionists on the implementation of various nutrition strategies. I undertook research at CDC to study the latest in training methods. I presented the concept of distance education and the capability of downlinking the training to states. I was charged with developing a series of training programs for nutritionist via distance education. I embarked on this work not knowing in detail the amount of work involved in developing the program and coordinating the downlink sites. I did not know that the Branch Chief would leave in the middle of the project. The support from the Division was very limited after he left the Division. As the project manager, I worked with the CDC distance education staff to develop the script, worked with the guest presenters to identify and coordinate the vignettes, and arranged for the call-ins on the day of production. Among the topics for this series was: *Nutrition: Making a Difference in Media, Supermarkets, Worksites and Schools* were among the topics for the series. *Nutrition:*

Making a Difference Media was acknowledged as a winner of a CDC Academy Award for Distant Education Training.

My only regret about the series program was I did not get an opportunity to produce, *Nutrition: Making a Different in Churches*. Dr. John Hatch from North Carolina had written the script for me. Dr. Hatch developed the first *Hypertension Program in Black Churches*. I felt this program would have been more sustainable in communities of colors. But with the increase in cost to produce and downlinks on the rise, CDC ran out of funding before the Church Program.

By far, this project was my mountainous and most challenging project at CDC. As the Project Manager, I would provide the directions and make the final decisions. As an example, these are some obstacles that I had to work thorough with the project. I shared with the artist that I did not like the art work for the lunch box and the artist became very upset because I gave my comments. A co-worker, desiring to take charge of the project continually plotted to disrupt communications and create negative reflections on my management style. But still, I prevailed.

CDC continued to provide me with exciting experiences. One such experience was a partnership with USDA-Beltsville Human Nutrition Research Center under the leadership of Dr. Ellen Harris. Several federal agencies collaborated under a Memorandum of Understanding to provide leadership and training for ten years to Historically Black Colleges and Universities, Food and Nutrition Department professors and students. Well of course, Southern University System, Baton Rouge, LA was one of the universities. Our program was called the Summer Institute and it provided professors and students with an opportunity to learn about public health, chronic disease programs, national and local community programs, surveillance programs, and evaluation tools. In addition, we all had the experience of our first International Nutrition Conference in Durban, South Africa. I presented a poster exhibit at the Nutrition Conference.

My next challenging and demanding project was the coordination for the development of the first national adolescent nutrition and physical activity tool. This project came about because of the request of Shirley Watkins, Under Secretary for Food, Nutrition, and Consumer Services at US Department of Agriculture. Mrs. Watkins and Bill Dietz, Director, Division of Nutrition, Physical Activity, and Obesity formed a Memorandum of Understanding to address the nutritional and physical activity requirements of adolescents in the US. With the data identifying the problems, educational and training tools were needed. I was assigned along with Refilwe Moeti, Physical Activity Consultant in the Division of Nutrition, Physical Activity and Obesity to spearhead this project. CDC contracted with the California Adolescent Nutrition and Fitness Program, under the leadership of the Executive Director, Arnell Hinkle, MPH, RD to develop the tool. This project was coordinated with USDA- Food and Nutrition Services, 100 Black Men of America, and the Boys and Girls Clubs of America. The tool that was developed was entitled, "Nutrition and Physical Activity the 100 Way" and the 100 Black Men of America provided training to their Chapters around the United States on the implementation of the program. USDA later modified the tool to be used by Child Care Centers.

Overseas Assignments

As a young woman, who had hardly traveled in the past; I applied and was accepted in the International Experience and Technical Assistance (IETA) Program. IETA is a developmental training program for Federal public health employees offered by the Center for Global Health at CDC. At the end of the course, a supervised short term (twelve-week minimum) overseas assignment with an international public health program is negotiated. An assignment is made based on skills and the needs of the program. Dar es Salaam, Tanzania here I come! I researched this country and was told by a colleague that Tanzania would be an excellent country for my experience. I was awed by the thought of going there. I had communicated by email with two staff members and was certain of two things before leaving for my assignment:

1. My living accommodations were in a downtown hotel suite and that this was a fairly safe place to live.
2. I would get to embrace my African heritage. When I compare the feeling of leaving home for Indianapolis for 6 months with that of Africa for 3 months, there was truly a different feeling. My heart was happy that I would finally get to Tanzania to work and have this experience of being involved with the Health Ministry, Embassy, and the local people.

CDC Tanzania Director of HIV and Annie Carr

I did not know what my daily experience/workday would be like. My first day assignment was traveling with a coworker and driver to a village about 2 hours away from Dar es Salaam. On the sides of the country road in June, everything was green and you could see people gardening. Life was slow outside of the city. Once in the village, all the dirt roads looked the same. I wondered how one finds their way in the day or at night. The village had no electricity.

Students from Historically Black Colleges and Universities were coming soon, and we were to identify safe living arrangements. Within weeks, the students arrived and they lived in the same hotel with me. However, their work assignments were throughout the country. I worked with them on their living and travel arrangements to and from Dar es Salaam for various monthly meetings.

I had heard about Zanzibar. So for my first weekend, arrangements were made for my trip to Zanzibar, transportation to the airport, ticket for the 15 minute flight, car and driver to take me to a hotel in Sandstone. I just had to give my credit card. I saw my name when I walked off the plane. My travel guide was excellent. He explained the various tour options and I selected what I wanted to do. The driver drove to this lovely hotel in the city of Sandstone on the ocean. The driver stated, "You know, President Clinton stayed at this hotel." My room was simply elegant; mahogany four post bed and mosquito nets surrounding the complete bed from top to floor. The view of the Indian Ocean was gorgeous! Sitting in the hotel restaurant for dinner was like something you see in the movies. Strong wind, stutters hitting the walls, the sound of the ocean waves hitting land, and the lanterns dimming inside by the wind. Was I dreaming?

Sandstone reminded me of the French Quarters in New Orleans with the narrow streets and two -story French architecture. However, the streets are narrower in Sandstone.

The Spice Farm tour was the highlight of my trip to Zanzibar. This may be because I use spices in cooking and I was interested in seeing how these spices and condiments grow. Maybe, I could grow some of the spices in USA.

During my fourth week in Dar es Salaam, I served as hostess for a cadre of heads of public health programs from Historically Black Colleges and Universities during their visit to our Tanzania office. What a surprise! Dr. Yvonne Bronner, PhD, RD, one of my dear friends from Morgan State University, Baltimore, Maryland and a member of the Food and Nutrition Section of American Public Health Association was one of the professors. I went out of my way to make the stay and learning experiences a titanic voyage for seven days.

My major project in Tanzania was to develop a training program on how to be a project officer. I developed training notebooks and tapes and presented on how to be an effective Project Officer for the Tanzania Project Officers working on HIV Programs. My college Layout and Design Class for food service kitchens paid off, as I read blue prints for the expansion of a new building at CDC Tanzania Office. I attended weekly construction meetings to review timelines, materials needed, work progress and any other problems.

A highlight for the Fourth of July celebration was receiving a personal invitation from the Ambassador of Tanzania inviting me to his home for a USA celebration. His quarters were lovely, decorated with a lot of Tanzanian wood and photos of himself with the current USA administration including the President.

Cameroon

Doula, Cameroon was my second overseas assignment. I was the Acting Deputy of Operations for eight weeks. My flight was into Yaoundé, Cameroon and I spent the night at a local hotel and traveled to Doula the next morning. The trip was around three hours, 15 minutes with a lot of local traffic in various small towns on the main highway. We had to travel in the day time because there were no street lights. My experience was in a small town off the ocean. The countryside was beautiful with banana trees growing for Dole and the ocean side providing plentiful fresh fish. On this side of the country the soil was very rich with many local farmers growing garlic, corn, pineapple, greens, plantains and potatoes. The women did a lot of farming in the area. I remember purchasing corn from the side of the highway and a woman made the sale. Mango trees were in just about everyone's yard. An afternoon outing to the ocean included eating grilled fresh fish, seasoned and mopped with herbs sauces, and grilled plantains. Experiencing this local culture at mealtime was so pleasurable that I learned to prepare native dishes using palm oil with the homeowner next door. I remember sharing with the homeowner that I like my plantain to turn yellow and get dark and she told me, "…that is too much sugar when they are dark; we prefer to eat green plantain."

I remember going to Yaoundé to the Embassy to look at a new office facility. Well, on our way the bridge was closed in one area and we had to take a small canoe to cross the river; the car was put on some type of raft. We all made it in one piece. On our return trip home the bridge was repaired.

I made a statement to my driver one morning on my way to work, "I wish it would have rained last night." He stated to me, "Oh no, don't wish that for us at night. This is the time that my family…We are mugged in our places." I just said, "Oh my goodness!" I didn't ask any questions and never made a comment about rain again.

I just loved being in Doula, Cameroon. I think it was because of the ocean and the fresh produce. I also remember taking walks every morning before getting ready for my driver to take me to work.

This trip to Cameroon was difficult to negotiate with the Division management in my CDC Atlanta office. They did not want to approve my accepting this special assignment even though I had been trained to do this type of work. Special written request had to be made for me to take this assignment. Basically, it took several weeks of negotiating for me to be approved. Yet I prevailed.

The Road of Hard Knocks Traveled - Only the Strong Survive

As a Registered Dietitian, and as an African American Dietitian, I can say the journey through my career has been an interesting one. I've been the first African American, Registered Dietitian to be employed by the Indiana Department of Education, the first Registered Dietitian/Nutritionist to be employed by the Indiana State Health Department of Health and the first Public Health Nutritionist at CDC in the National Center for Chronic Disease Prevention. I've been the Food and Nutrition Chair for American Public Health Association.

There have been many experiences that I've had in my various work settings, some of which have offered me great opportunities and others that have been quite challenging. One must be astute in identifying which is which.

Sometimes assessing my qualifications and years of experience with those of my peers with less experience has been difficult for some employers. The assessments have been put on the same level as those with less experience. There have been times when staff and co-workers wouldn't share work information or special details with me. In some meetings I have been invisible, and when I offered suggestions they were ignored. Yet, someone else in the same meeting would say the same thing and suddenly it was a great idea. Often, the rules were not the same when it came to my receiving "time off" and "comp time." My job performance had to be over and beyond the call of duty to get an outstanding on an evaluation, and if I was a leader in the work place, it wouldn't be recognized. I remember giving a Center level presentation, one of my co-workers stated, "You sound like you were preaching." When you are working on a committee and it's your time to lead the group, the support is not the same.

In spite of everything, I've looked for opportunities to be involved. During my many years as a Registered Dietitian/ Nutritionist I have had many accomplishments of which I am very proud.

I've mentored many students in the field of dietetics, students attending HBCUs, high school students and co-workers just needing encouragement.

I have conducted cooking classes (vegetables and fruits only) for seniors at the Walker Center and Bethesda Church in DeKalb County. I also volunteer in my community working on various health issues that are prevalent among African Americans.

Coordinated the American Diabetes Association booth
at the "Sister Only Conference", Atlanta, GA

My professional achievements are as follows:

- Winner of the Catherine Cowell Award from the Food and Nutrition Section of American Public Health Association.
- Organizer of a special community event in Atlanta, Georgia for the Food and Nutrition Section of the American Public Health Association. This event recognized Faye Wong, MPH, RD as the incoming President of the American Public Health Association and Frances Cook, MS, RD for her outstanding work as the Georgia Nutrition Director.
- Chair of the Food and Nutrition Section of the American Public Health Association, pioneering the development of the Mission and Vision Statement for the section.

Travel – See the World

Independently, I have traveled and connected with the Motherland of Africa (Ghana, Kenya, Ethiopia, Egypt, South Africa and Morocco) and I have learned about cooking styles and the types of foods that are grown in these countries. My Holy Land trip was with my Daddy and Auntie and one of my most rewarding experiences was to see their amazement and hear their comments. I remember my Daddy stated, "I never thought in my life time that I would get an opportunity to travel to this part of the world." At the time Daddy was 78 years old. I had heard Daddy talk so much about the Jordan River, Gaza Wall, Jerusalem, and the Dead Sea. It was from this trip that I learned to add whole cardamom to my coffee beans and grind just like they do in the Holy Land.

I was told, "You must take a Greek Island Cruise because people in the USA only think about the Caribbean cruises." I decided first to see Athens, Greece and then take the Greek Island Cruise. It was amazing and I had the opportunity to put my feet on Turkish soil.

With my nephew being in the military, I had my first opportunity to visit with him overseas in Germany. Using Germany as my base location, I ventured off after one day by train for a one-day excursion full of excitement to the Netherlands. Over the weekend, I used my 15-day Euro Train pass to begin my travel to Paris, London, Brussels and Rome. My second overseas visit with him was to Seoul, South Korea. My first five days of this experience were planned by the American Korean Family Support Program. We toured, experiencing the culture, eating and shopping in some of the best locations in the city. While waiting for some special military ID on post, I saw on the bulletin board this advertisement about a four day trip to Hong Kong, China at an unbelievable cost. My first thought was, you will never get this kind of price to travel to China again! So,

I decided I must see Hong Kong for four days. I remember shopping and walking the streets feeling like a giant in comparison to the local people. I could not help but be noticed being African American and 5 feet 6 inches.

One of my latest trips was to Australia and New Zealand. I must have a fascination with cities located at the seaside. The seafood, fresh fruits and vegetables were expensive but very tasty. I knew that there are a lot of wines imported from Australia, but to see so many wineries that are locally owned and that sell only to locals and tourists traveling in the area was amazing.

This part of my story is simply to share that we learn so much in traveling and seeing how others are living happy lives in their countries. We all eat fruit, vegetables, fish, shrimp, crab, oysters, meat, grains and baked goods. But each part of the world has a unique style in preparing foods according to their culture. The spices and condiments used will make a difference in the taste of the food.

Pearls of Wisdom

Having accomplished much in my career as a Registered Dietitian, there are some pearls of wisdom I would like to pass on to those of you who might not be sure about what you want your own career path to be. The list is not in any particular order, but each one of them can work well in your life:

- Make sure that your job is fulfilling.
- Be true to yourself.
- Always reach back to help others.
- Learn the office politics wherever you go. This is something that you are not taught in the class room.

- Respect others.
- Realize that you must have a pleasing personality to work with people.
- The field of Dietetics is very broad; define your best skills and explore what works best for you.
- Be involved in professional, community, and civic organizations.

Classmates from Southern University, Baton Rouge, LA attending an American Dietetic Association meeting (Registered Dietitians; Eardell Ducre, Annie Carr, Ruth London, Barbara McKnight, and Florentine Green)

- Be well rounded and grounded.
- Listen and learn before you speak.

Last, but not least, enjoy your life in the dietetics field or whatever field you select!

Work is what we do to make a living, so make it enjoyable and keep people around you that love and respect you.

I must leave you with these wise words suggested to me by Auntie as I was preparing for a presentation at Southern University, Baton Rouge, Louisiana for the graduating dietetic interns. Auntie said, "After you read the verses, stand for a second, then sit down."

Trust in the Lord with all thine heart: and lean not unto thine own understanding.

In all thy ways acknowledge him, and he shall direct thy path. Proverbs 3: 5 - 6

FATHER KNOWS BEST

Frances Hanks Cook

The autumn leaves danced around my swollen, ashy knees as I loaded the barrel with the last heavy bundle of peanuts and cotton. "Oh, thank God crop season has ended!" my four siblings and I joyously exclaimed. I was so happy that I jumped and skipped through the multi-colored leaves and became even more joyous when I heard the sound of a school bell ringing from across the field. For I knew that tomorrow, I would be able to go to school. Although I had already missed the first two weeks of school due to the cotton and peanut harvest season falling within the first two weeks of the school year, I was anxious to remove the heavy weight of that brown burlap sack from my arms and replace it with my school books.

As I listened to that school bell ring I forgot all about the dark-brown glaze that the July's heat had left on my pecan-tan face. Yes, the sound of that school bell was very comforting to me. For every chime that echoed through that field, I realized that there was an opportunity for me to plant seeds beyond the fertile ground I stood on. For every chime that rang, I realized that I would be successful and that my education would take me to places where the greenest of corn could take root and courageously grow.

Early Life

I was born in Fort Gaines, Georgia the first of five children. In Fort Gaines Georgia, I grew up on a 500-acre family owned farm which my great grandfather purchased following the abolishment of slavery. My great grandfather was a very ambitious man for his time. From the moment that he obtained his freedom, he saved the money that he earned while share-cropping for the privileged whites of his community and he purchased the deed and ownership of the place that I call home. His daily devotion to his agrarian work is the inheritance that sustained my family including my parents and four siblings. In essence, his determination and relentless commitment to be successful in the midst of many adversities, provided our daily work, taught us a strong work ethic, and the value of a dollar.

Living on the family farm, which my great grandfather purchased after the abolishment of slavery, required my entire family to be a "Sower" of seed and a "Reaper" of harvest. Let me tell you, the hardest work I have ever known in my life was preparing and harvesting vegetables, cotton, peanuts, and corn. Nonetheless, in that same breath I must say that due to the blessings from our harvest, I cannot recall a time that I went to bed with an empty stomach. My father would often say "Frances Ruth, if you work hard you can make a decent and honest living for yourself." My father was a very strong, healthy six feet tall man who never met a stranger. He had an infectious personality and a booming, loud voice which you could hear at least a mile away. My four siblings and I often joked that he used his "Hog Calling" voice with everyone he encountered.

My mother however was an extremely quiet, nurturing homemaker whose soft-spoken voice matched her petite 95-pound frame. At the end of a long day working on the farm, she would have prepared a healthy dinner primarily from our "rock star" vegetable garden of collards, mustards, turnip greens, cabbage, and sweet potatoes. As my mother prepared our meals she often sweetly hummed beautiful gospel tunes such as "Amazing Grace." She was a spirit-filled woman who truly loved the Lord and she adored her children. Mother had a pomegranate tree in our back yard that she delighted in and always enjoyed sharing the fruit with family, friends and neighbors. After eating so many of the pomegranate seeds (arils), we began to wonder what else we could do with this fruit. We learned through information from the Pomegranate Council how to juice the fruit, use it in recipes and in holiday decorations. That tree is still in the back yard and bearing fruit. Today, when we meet for family gathering there is at least one dish containing pomegranate.

Pomegranate Council – Dijon chicken with Pomegranate Glaze

1 chicken (about 3 lbs.)
Dijon mustard
2 cups pomegranate juice
1 tablespoon brown sugar
2 teaspoons soy sauce

Split the chicken in half, brush heavily with Dijon mustard, and roast in a 500°F oven for 30 minutes. Pour pomegranate juice into a large skillet, and reduce it by half. Stir in brown sugar and soy sauce. Boil briefly, then pour over the chicken. Reduce the temperature to 300°F and bake for an additional 15 minutes.

Nutrition Facts Per Serving:
¼ chicken: Calories 521; Fat 10g; Cholesterol 107mg; Sodium 420mg; Carbohydrates 71g; Protein 36g.

My parents instilled a value system that included the importance of Christ in our lives, hard work, determination, integrity and a college education as core values to which I ascribe today. The generational roots of my ancestors as tillers of the soil, planters of seed, and harvesters of bounty are the inspiration for my siblings and me to find the path that led to personal fulfillment. The following narrative is my career development story of sowing many seeds as a successful nutritionist and earning noteworthy accolades and awards by helping others.

Role Models and Mentors

While parents provide the foundation for values through parental direction, discipline, and guidance; role models and mentors are the angels commissioned to clarify and uphold the vision. They provide the encouragement that says, not only will dreams come true, but the horizon is broader than anyone can imagine. Of course, as a child growing up, my vision and access to mentors and role models were limited to the professionals to whom I was exposed. School teachers were the most common in our community. My homeroom teacher, Thomas I. Johnson, and his wife, Mildred, who was my Home Economics teacher, had a great influence on my education and academic collegiate career.

As a student in Mrs. Johnson's Home Economics class, I was introduced to the science of food and nutrition and home management. I found food and nutrition more attractive and fascinating to study. As a dedicated student eager to learn, the Johnsons were instrumental in my application to Tuskegee Institute, now named Tuskegee University, because of its reputation for high caliber training in Food and Nutrition and the Five-Year Work Plan. It offered an intensive design for a five-year baccalaureate program instead of the usual four-year program. As a student in the program, it provided part-time work on campus along with a reduced course load. I was paid with vouchers which were submitted to the accounting office to pay my tuition each semester. In my personal observation, I realized that my social and work management skills improved at a very fast rate. This was due to the high expectations for me to be a productive employee as well as maintain a three-point grade average. I experienced success in meeting these criteria.

Through my diligence and dedicated application as a student, my life began to develop with leaps and bounds. After my junior year, my college advisor paved the way for me to perform a summer internship at Beth Israel Hospital (BI) in Boston. The experience was excellent in offering direct observation of the professionals in action. It provided clarity for defining my professional goal and strengthened my future application for a dietetic internship at Beth Israel.

Benefits of Serving in an Internship

As you can see from following this narrative that my life has come a long way from the farm. In just five years, I have a bachelor's degree from an environment that has not only prompted my maturity and scholarship on its college campus, enhanced my professional knowledge and afforded exposure to nutrition and dietetics at BI. This experience also provided the opportunity for travel, and residential life in two states beyond my birthplace. In addition, my internships paid a stipend to cover personal care items. Boston was truly a place of historical significance, ethnic diversity, and medical achievement. BI was a Harvard teaching facility which made it rich with excitement in the pursuit of medical knowledge.

The staff was open to innovative concepts and allowed dietetic interns to be creative in implementing new ideas. We were given guidelines rather than dictums and allowed to think "outside the box", as long as it met the desired outcomes. My most enjoyable rotation was the outpatient-clinic. This rotation provided an opportunity to follow the patients after discharge from the hospital and to respond to all the questions regarding their nutrition plan. The joint classes with Brigham Women Hospital and Massachusetts General Hospital interns were great for social development, networking and gaining knowledge and experience.

I have very fond memories of the home that BI designated as the dietetic interns' residence that was about one-quarter of a mile from the hospital. Our house mother lived there as well and truly was our "mother away from home." She was committed, caring, and loving to each of the twelve interns in our class. We worked long, hard hours, and studied long hours once we returned to our intern residence. For special celebrations, such as Christmas, Thanksgiving, Patriot day, and so on, we would meet in the lobby area for fun, food, and fellowship. After successful completion of my dietetic internship, I received my Registered Dietitian Designation and began work as a clinical dietitian, my first full-time employment experience, at New York University Medical Center. This relationship spanned five successful years.

Scholarship, Career, and Professional Development

As I continued to gain more professional exposure and academic knowledge as a clinical dietitian at NYU Medical Center, my interest evolved to Public Health/Community Nutrition. The public health, population-based approach is distinguished from the clinical or one-on-one patient care approach that I was currently practicing.

The community rather than the individual is seen as the "patient." On many occasions, I had given diet instructions to clients during the interval between discharge from the hospital and often while being wheeled to the elevator to depart for home. I made a decision to enter graduate school part-time at NYU. Tuition fees were one of the fringe benefits of an NYU Medical Center employee. I clearly could see that an advanced degree was the next significant step up the career ladder to enhance my professional credibility in the fields of nutrition and dietetics. So for the next three years I juggled the often difficult, competing demands of a full-time job and part-time graduate student. Fortunately, my father's sister "Aunt Marie" lived in Brooklyn New York, and she provided me with a home away from home. The love and support I received from Aunt Marie and her family sustained me as I pursued my professional and academic dreams. I have very fond memories of sitting at that unleveled table in my Aunt Marie's small kitchen, savoring those delicious meals, especially those sweet potatoes pies, homemade yeast rolls and pound cake. Below is Aunt Marie's pound cake recipe. Certainly this was a very challenging, yet sacred period of my professional journey.

Aunt Marie's Pound Cake

2 3/4 cups of sugar
1 1/4 cups of butter, softened
1 teaspoon vanilla
5 eggs
3 cups all-purpose flour
1 teaspoon baking powder
1/4 teaspoon salt
1 cup Carnation evaporated milk

Heat oven to 350 degrees. Grease and flour a 10-inch tube pan; set aside. In a large bowl, cream the butter, sugar and eggs on low speed, scraping bowl constantly for 30 seconds. Beat on high speed for 5 minutes while scraping the bowl occasionally. In another bowl, sift the flour, salt and baking powder. Add the flour in small batches to the creamed mixtures alternately with the milk, beginning and ending with the flour.

Add vanilla and blend well. Pour batter into prepared pan and place in the oven. Bake at 350 degrees for 1 hour and 30 minutes or until top springs back when touched.

Let cake stand for 20 minutes in the pan to cool. Run a knife around the edges and remove cake carefully to a rack. Yield 16 slices

One slice: Calories 496; Fat 24g; Cholesterol 112mg; Sodium 213 mg; Carbohydrate 66g; Protein 6g.

After completing my master's degree in nutrition from NYU, I worked sixteen months as a community nutritionist with the New York City Maternal and Infant Care Project. My assignments were at the Brooklyn and Bronx clinics. My role was to educate our clientele on nutrition using primarily three methods, one-to-one counseling, group classes, and food demonstrations. I was committed to helping people become healthier through foods by assisting them to be wiser about their choices, so they could grow to be more active in their own health care. One of my greatest challenges in this role was learning to communicate with the clients who were Spanish-speaking.

Unfortunately for me, due to a heavy Spanish-speaking client-base, the only interpreter was also challenged to provide adequate assistance to staff that served in a variety of roles (nurses, doctors, administrators, social workers) that all required interpretation services. It was during this time that I met Dr. Catherine Cowell who proved to be an inspirational mentor. Through her insight and knowledge, she guided me into considering other opportunities in Public Health Nutrition. As a result of this relationship, I was honored to receive the "Catherine Cowell Award" in Public Health Nutrition at the 2010 American Public Health Association annual meeting in Atlanta, Georgia.

In 1971, I began to contemplate and conduct a self-assessment and evaluation to renew my career goals. Within that space of thoughts and emotions, I began to yearn to return south so that I could be more readily accessible and supportive to my parents. Armed with my master's degree, I shared my renewed vision with a very dear college classmate and special friend, Joyce McKay; she suggested that I contact the Child Health Nutrition consultant with the Georgia Department of Public Health. Joyce had worked with this consultant on several Maternal and Child Health Nutrition projects. Through that referral, I was hired by Dr. Albert Schoenbucker, a highly respected obstetrician. In October 1972, I relocated to Atlanta, Georgia, and joined the Georgia Department of Public Health as the first African American state wide Maternal Nutrition Consultant. Dr. Schoenbucker put me on notice that there could be many challenges and indeed there were. He was always there to provide his unfailing support.

During this time, the infrastructure for delivering preventive health care services was through the local health departments in Georgia's 159 counties. The staffing pattern in the local health departments were primarily registered nurses and clerical staff. Therefore, the Child Health Nutrition Consultant and I had to develop, implement and monitor statewide minimum nutrition guidelines and standards in nutrition counseling for the public health nurses. These minimum standards provided a basic level of knowledge to assist the nurses with disseminating accurate nutrition information to their clients who were primarily pregnant women, infants and children. As state level nutrition consultants, we accomplished this through statewide Maternal and Child Health in-service training programs, site visits, newsletters, training manuals, and nutrition education materials.

In 1976, I was promoted to a newly established state- wide office and position as the Director of the Office of Nutrition. The mission of this office was to provide state leadership for achieving optimal nutrition health for Georgia's Maternal and Child Health population. This included the Women, Infant and Children program (WIC). Primary strategies for executing this mission involved the development and the implementation of a statewide public health system that would provide nutrition services and information to Georgia's citizens. This system involved policymaking, statewide planning and evaluation, management, supervision and fiscal control. Program planning included a population-based approach to address the complexity of obesity and chronic disease prevention. As part of the approach, we built partnerships and collaborations between public health, the community, schools, worksites, and the private sector.

Clearly, my role as the Director for the Office of Nutrition presented some of the most challenging seasons of my career and when I received opposition from former colleagues who felt they should have been promoted to this position, I recalled something my father always told me, "Frances Ruth, in this life people may knock you down but you are responsible for getting back up". And indeed, that is what I did.

Despite a lack of funding and other limitations I, along with a highly dedicated state-wide committee, successfully met the goal of building an effective Nutrition program through creative programming and networking. We made nutrition an integral component of state and community health agencies. It also was during this time that I met my husband, Edmond Cook, who has been so supportive of me during my professional journey.

One of the critical factors that made the development and implementation of the Nutrition Program very challenging was the limited availability of trained nutrition practitioners in the rural area of the state. The public health nurses embraced the mission of the Nutrition program; however, they were not interested in the management of the certification component of the Nutrition program. As previously mentioned, there were only two nutrition consultants at the state level and two in the local health departments across the state (DeKalb and Ware counties) in 1976. Added to the enormous task in the development and implementation of the Nutrition Program was Georgia's landmass of 58,483 square miles coupled with the fact that 78% of the state was rural and sparsely populated.

Despite these obstacles, we organized a steering committee, which consisted of district medical health directors, nurses, nutritionists and clerks, to develop a plan to implement the Nutrition program statewide. During this implementation process four critical areas were defined and developed. These areas included; (1) ensuring that we had the basic core staff to manage the program at the state and the 19 local public health districts, (2) developing a nutrition staffing pattern to include job descriptions, recruitment, orientation and training procedures, (3) providing program monitoring and (4) evaluating the Nutrition program to ensure compliance with state and federal rules and regulations.

It was my personal and professional mission to ensure that the Nutrition program effectively met the needs of the underserved populations. It brings me great elation to share that we were quite successful in completing and implementing these four strategies and the Georgia WIC program was implemented, district by district, and was statewide by 1980. The WIC caseload and nutrition staff continued to grow and after ten years, the state and district staff had grown from four nutritionists in 1976 to 190 nutritionists by May 2007. As a result of this work, I was appointed to serve on the National Advisory Council on Maternal Infant and Fetal Nutrition.

Major Challenges and Accomplishments

Many fascinating stories and challenges paved the road of my career since arriving in the State of Georgia and developing the Nutrition program. My primary challenge was that the local agencies had limited nutrition staff, limited experience in community/public health, and only 26% of the staff was registered dietitians/ nutritionists (RDN). Our assessment of the local nutrition staff revealed that they did not pursue internships or graduate school because of low grade point averages, limited intern slots, finances, geographic, and personal barriers. We considered several strategies to address these concerns. One approach was to develop a Community-Based Dietetic Internship accredited through the Commission on Accreditation for Dietetic Education or CADE (now called the Accreditation Council for Education in Nutrition and Dietetic or ACEND).

The planning committee that developed this self-study included state and local nutrition staff, university faculty, preceptors, health directors, and potential interns. This committee composition was vital to securing the buy-in of all stakeholders, especially the supervisors of the potential interns. Supervisors were the gate keepers to release interns from their jobs for the 20-hour a week participation in off-site experiences in order to achieve basic dietetic competencies.

Throughout my career, it had always been a personal desire to help others reach their professional and career goals. This internship program provided a means for the state and local nutritionists to reach their professional goals. It was paramount that at least 60% of the required program experience be conducted in the community where the interns resided and worked. The benefits to the state agency included:

- A partnership with community agencies
- Continuity of patient care from the hospitals to the community
- Facilitation of recruitment efforts for public health nutritionists
- Innovative projects initiated by interns/employees

We developed and submitted in 1991, a proposal for a Community-Based Dietetic Internship to ACEND. We received approval from ACEND and Georgia became the second state agency (following Virginia) to have an accredited internship in a public health state agency. Prior to this time, dietetic Internships were traditionally managed in hospitals and universities. In April 1992, we accepted our first four employee/interns. This was certainly one of my crowning professional accomplishments in Nutrition and Dietetic.

When I retired in 2007, one hundred and fifty (150) employees (public health nutritionists) had completed the dietetic internship with a passing rate of 80% for first- time takers of the National Registration Examination. Demographically, 65% of the graduates were White, 30% African American, 3% Hispanic and 2% others. The competency level of nutritionists for the delivery of sound nutrition service throughout the state had increased immensely; registered dietitians/ nutritionists on staff increased by 60%, and 50% of internship graduates had received employment promotions. Personally, this produced a sense of gratitude, reward and accomplishment. This experience caused me to reflect on a statement I often make "Leadership means stewardship, which means leaving a place in better shape than when you started" Above all, when graduates of the internship program approach me at nutrition meetings, by telephone, e-mail and express their appreciation for helping them advance their nutrition careers and credentials that is the icing on the cake. It is truly gratifying to see and hear of how they have become excellent practitioners and leaders involved in professional activities, and happy with the choices they have made. For it was during this season of my professional journey that I proudly took the scenic route to see the fruit of my work.

Other Opportunities and Rewards

The directorship of the Georgia State Office of Nutrition afforded other opportunities for professional growth and affiliation. I was appointed Program Chair for the 63rd Nutrition Conference of the American Dietetic Association (now the Academy of Nutrition and Dietetics) when the meeting was held in Atlanta, Georgia for the first time, October 5-9, 1980. The opportunity to serve in this capacity exposed me to all the logistics and techniques in planning, implementing and evaluating a national meeting. This experience served me well through-out my career.

Serving as a program reviewer on site visits for the Commission on Accreditation for Dietetic Education or CADE (now ACEND) provided an opportunity to review many universities' dietetic programs and dietetic internships. This experience stimulated ideas for improving Georgia's community-based internship and offered valuable insight on what to expect during Georgia's Internship program review process.

I had the pleasure of serving on the Item Writing Review Committee for the community nutrition questions on the National Registration

Examination for Dietitians. This enhanced my understanding of the process used to develop valid and plausible questions.

Another rewarding experience was when my Office received a grant from The Centers for Disease Control and Prevention to implement a state-based Nutrition and Physical Activity Program. This program addressed the problem of obesity and other related chronic diseases. The focus areas were Healthy Eating, Physical Activity, TV viewing and Breastfeeding. The grant required a comprehensive and population-based approach to address the complexity of obesity prevention. It was mandated that we create a partnership between public health, the community, schools, worksites, and the private sector.

We recognized during the implementation of this obesity project that the nutrition practitioners gained noteworthy visibility with the general public and other health professionals. They came to recognize both the important role nutrition plays in health and the need for advice from food and nutrition experts. It also was gratifying to observe the obesity initiative being embraced by the White House through the aggressive leadership of our former First Lady Michelle Obama and her "Let's Move" Program designed to address the epidemic of childhood obesity within a generation.

As State Nutrition Director, I represented Georgia at the meetings and boards of the Association of State and Territorial Public Health Nutrition Directors or ASTPHND (now called the Association of State Public Health Nutritionists). During my tenure, the members of the association were director of nutrition programs and services in the public health agencies of the 50 states, the District of Columbia, and the five territories. The exchanges with other states agency directors provided numerous opportunities to improve program management and services. During my first meeting of ASTPHND,

I met Anita Owen, who was the Chief Nutritionist for the State of Arizona. (She became the 61st President of American Dietetic Association.) I continued to learn much from Anita as I consulted with her on many projects.

I became the second African American president of the Association of State Public Health Nutritionists for 1996-1997. I encountered many challenges, through it all, and I always remembered what my father taught me, "Stay focused on your mission and surround yourself with those who will support you." And indeed that is what I did. During my tenure as president, we published "Moving to the Future: Developing Community-Based Nutrition Services". It explains how to plan, gain approval, secure funding, and execute the four major steps necessary to develop and implement successful nutrition interventions. These steps include conducting a community assessment, determining health priorities, writing goals and objectives, implementing the interventions, and monitoring and evaluating the intervention. Georgia was one of the states that participated in the review and testing of this handbook prior to publication. Through state and local training, consultation and site visits this planning process was implemented in Georgia's nineteen Public Health districts.

I was appointed by the governor to serve on the Georgia Board of Examiners of Licensed Dietitians as a public health representatives from 2008-2013. Major responsibilities included compliance with the rules of the board, a review and evaluation to ensure that all Georgia Licensed Dietitian (GLD) applicants complied with all licensure requirements, continuing professional education, ethics of Dietitians and provisional permits. This highlighted the State's goal which is to protect the public and ensure the delivery of sound nutrition information.

The opportunity to serve as an Adjunct Professor under the leadership of Dr. Sara Hunt, the first director of the Food and Nutrition Department at Georgia State University was a very valuable experience. Again, this was another opportunity to be a part of building the next generation of strong nutrition leaders.

Words to the Next Generation

My words of wisdom to the younger generation are to always plant seeds of excellence! To recognize that even though you may not feel content or experience a sense of accomplishment within your current career endeavors, there is an opportunity awaiting you that would not be available if you did not have the strong foundation set in place by the most difficult, challenging times of your career. These difficult phases of your career will be the bridge to get you where you want to go. So, don't burn your bridges. As my third- grade-educated father so eloquently put it, "Frances Ruth, even though it seems like that tomato plant takes a long time to grow, just know that there is growth occurring beneath the soil – in a place that the human eye cannot see." To put it simply, I would encourage the younger generations to know that with every life experience they are being prepared for "Greatness." Finally, I encourage the next generation to never stop learning because education is a life-long journey.

I would like to strongly encourage the next generation to reach down and help someone else along the way. Life is filled with benefits and caveats; you never know when you may need someone to reach down and out to you.

Just as Mr. and Mrs. Johnson, encouraged me to enter the Tuskegee University Food and Nutrition Bachelors Program, and Dr. Albert

Schoenbucker, the obstetrician provided me with guidance during my experiences as the first African American nutrition consultant in the state of Georgia, my hope is that, you, too, will encourage and guide others during your career and life journey.

In Closing

Retirement can cause you to resign from everything that is worthwhile in life or it can open up a new door in life. When I retired in 2007, I chose the latter. My living is renewed as I continue involvement in bible study and pursue career exploration in health and nutrition community initiatives. As stated earlier, my parents raised us in a Christian home and instilled Christian values to last a lifetime. It is only by the grace and mercy of the Creator that I have received these blessings in my personal and professional life.

Since retirement, I have almost completed the study of the entire bible through my church, Christian Fellowship Baptist church in College Park, Georgia and two International Bible Study groups, a Community Bible Study and Bible Study Fellowship. This has been a glorifying experience. It has deepened my faith and love for God. The Biblical scriptures remind us of humanity's concern about food throughout history. Feasts, famines, food as an expression of hospitality, laws pertaining to the use of food, and food as symbols are all recorded with some detail in the Bible.

It was the summer of 2013 and the weekend of our annual Hanks and Turner Family Reunion. As soon as I entered the city limits of Fort Gaines, Georgia and drove up the hill to the entry gates of the 500 acres of the farmland that my great grandfather purchased following the emancipation proclamation of 1863. I had one of Oprah's "Ah Ha!!!" moments. For this was the moment that I truly realized the fallacy of my previous belief that leaving home to pursue an education was my means to escape a life of working on the family farm. I now recognized that during my professional journey, I had actually mirrored the life work of my ancestors. For example, through my successful matriculation within the Tuskegee University Food and Nutrition bachelor's degree program and my internship at Beth Israel, I had to till the land. Through meeting the competing demands of working a full-time clinical dietitian job at the New York University Medical Center while completing my graduate studies at New York University, I had sowed the seeds, and through my work as the Director of the Office of Nutrition I had reached the harvest season of my professional journey whereby I harvested policies and programs to improve the health and well-being of the Maternal and Child Health population. Yes, very similar to my great grandfather, my life work as a Public Health Nutritionist provided nutritious foods to the tables of man-kind. At the core of my being, I am still the daughter of a farmer providing life-giving seeds to my community.

Finally, as mature adults my siblings and I have developed a profound appreciation for our laboring in the fields on our family farm and in tribute to our ancestors – my siblings and I constructed a portion of the family farmland into a respite and retreat area. There, we can truly appreciate the beauty of God's creation. There we can ensure that our family history, values, and traditions are not lost and there we can provide an opportunity for the next generation to literally travel the sacred paths of their ancestors.

It is my hope that during our family retreat gatherings on the farm, we will be reminded that we stand on the shoulders of our ancestors and that we are the proud inheritors of an African American tradition of praying, farming, struggling and accomplishing in the midst of adversity.

FRANCES HANKS COOK, MA, RDN, LD

2013 Hanks and Turner Reunion Family Tree

Entry Gate to Hanks and Turner Retreat. This
gate is in memory of our father

Lake View

Back of the Farmhouse

Patio and Porch

Side of the Farmhouse

Family Gathering Room

Family Gathering Room Fireplace

2013 Family Reunion Group (Frances Cook on right,
standing on the ground next to steps).

I WAS A TERROR

Catherine Cowell

That I refused to let others stop me on my road to being a model Public Health Nutritionist can be traced to my early childhood. I was a terror! And I paid the price. My older brother was the quiet type; he would never fight back. One day I looked out of the window of our house and saw some neighborhood boys ganging up on my brother. I went outside and beat them up; they had to pull me off them. As an adult I observed that some of the actions of my professional peers were obvious; others were subtle but carried the same negative message. Being determined to be successful I kept a positive attitude at all times and worked twice as hard to demonstrate my ability and commitment to the profession. Once I did that I concentrated on being productive as a professional, because no matter what I did I would never convince those with deep-seeded (planted early in life and is buried deep in the psych) cultural biases. I strongly felt and feel now that life is too short to engage all of one's mental and physical energy addressing racial bias.

My professional journey began with my family. I was the middle child with an older brother and younger sister. After my father passed when I was young my mother relocated from Norfolk, VA to Reading, PA. She worked full-time so I was given the responsibility for cooking dinner meals for the family after I came home from school. My brother and sister cleared the table and washed the dishes. After moving North my mother worked full time as a cook for many families. Fortunately, she worked for one wealthy family who treasured her cooking skills for making many of the traditional Pennsylvania Dutch dishes; i.e. shoo-fly pie, cinnamon buns, fasnachs (a type of doughnut associated with Lent), pot pies, souse and many other dishes. Perhaps the most treasured dish was her homemade pastas! As a result, we children benefitted by being driven to school on cold and snowy days.

My mother stressed the role of education, religion and the church in our lives. Indeed, she practiced what she preached—attending church every Sunday and engaging in church activities. She demonstrated what she believed. Every Saturday she spent cooking, especially baking bread and rolls for the week (plus a special treat of "sticky buns" for us) and the main dish for Sunday.

She cooked on a wood stove and would put her hand in the oven to determine the temperature. I almost flunked a course my freshman year at Hampton University for putting my hand in the oven instead of using a thermometer. After Sunday church and dinner it was off to either the library or museum. If there was a concert, poetry reading or play at church we would attend.

My mother also taught us how to make root beer. She would buy the extract at the grocery store to which we would add water, seal the bottle and let it sit for 48 hours. I will never forget the time my brother put in too much extract in the water and our Sunday treat exploded.

Schools we attended were predominately white (teachers and students), significantly of German descent and known as "PA Dutch." In fact, German was a second language especially in high school along with classes in Latin and French. I chose French because I felt I could pick up enough German from my classmates. There were only 3 African Americans in my high school of over 1,000.

About the time I was in 10th grade I decided I was going to college. A black physician, Dr. James Goodwin, Jr., opened one of the first medical practices in the city. Dr. Goodwin organized a scholarship club which encouraged black students to excel in high school and go to college. Modest financial assistance was offered. Club members were encouraged to visit black colleges before making a decision. I chose Hampton Institute (now University). This was the same college my brother attended before being drafted during World War II. I never regretted this choice since I was able to work and support myself while attending school.

I enrolled in Home Economics where I encountered faculty who were well-trained and provided guidance and counseling. It so happened that one of my counselors and instructors was Flemmie P. Kittrell who was both Dean of Women and an Instructor in the Department. Dr. Kittrell shared with her students a strong sense of the significant contributions they could make to society by working with culturally diverse families around home and family issues. She also shared experiences relative to her successful completion of a Ph.D. at Cornell University in 1935, the first black woman to do so. The recognition she received as a Home Economist impressed me.

I made the decision then and there that I too would focus in this field. Dr. Kittrell had a major in nutrition and minor in child development. While at Hampton she created and supported a course in child development and established a nursery school for young children and their families. This approach provided a bridge between theory in the classroom and practice at the nursery school. This fascinated me. Being in a college environment that included a focus on family was a continuation of my own family experiences—a positive reinforcement of what had been instilled by my mother.

I thoroughly enjoyed cooking family meals and didn't look at it as a task. I looked forward to cooking and watching my mother on Saturdays when she was cooking, especially making bread and other "goodies." Those observations along with other experiences and course work at Hampton confirmed a strong interest in food and nutrition, making the field of Home Economics my ultimate goal. As fate would have it one of the several jobs I had at Hampton was working in the dietary department at a local hospital. I observed how a hospital functioned and related to food service and nutrition for patients. This opportunity further supported my interest in food and nutrition.

After graduation from Hampton in January 1945, I went to New York City. There I applied for, and worked as counselor for the Children's Aid Society. I was assigned to an upstate residence that housed about 15 girls from Harlem referred by the Courts; they were roughly 12 to 17 years of age. As a counselor I quickly saw the need to involve the girls in preparing food, so I started a cooking class. Of all the other activities, the Cooking Class was the most popular and best-attended activity. While there I reflected on my future and made the decision to enroll in graduate school if I was to achieve my goal in life.

While attending Hampton University I learned about the dietetics profession. This was reinforced when I enrolled at the University of Connecticut at Storrs where I attended graduate school. But it was when I was still at Hampton that I became excited about concentrating on food and nutrition for families. With a broad background in Home Economics as my basis, I felt excited about the potential for working with families around food and nutrition.

At the University of Connecticut I majored in Home Economics and was guided by Dr. Martha Potgieter, Chairperson of the Department. Her focus was research on a range of food and nutrition issues, so I was comfortable in conducting research on the vitamin C content in four varieties of locally grown kale. As an alumnus of Teachers College, Columbia University, New York City, Dr. Potgieter took her graduate students to visit Teachers College and collaborate, when feasible, on research projects. This was a unique experience.

My first position in the field was as Laboratory Technician at Mt. Sinai Hospital in New York City where I was a member of a team that analyzed blood and urine samples from patients (children and adults) attending the first Nutrition Clinics established by the New York City Department of Health. These Nutrition Clinics established and headed by the late Dr. Norman Jolliffe probably were among the first ones in this country. Dr. Joliffe established a public health method to address the growing problems of obesity and coronary heart disease in the country. The first weight control clinic was established for over-weight adults in 1950 at one of the four nutrition clinics, New York City Department of Health. This was followed by men who were enrolled as members of the Anti-Coronary Club designed to reduce the risk of coronary heart disease. One result was the development of the Prudent Diet.

At Mt. Sinai Hospital one of my colleagues, a nutritionist resigned to accept a position with the Bureau of Nutrition as a Public Health Nutritionist. She was very excited once she started to work and contacted me to apply for a position because there were openings. She pursued me until I applied and was accepted as a Public Health Nutritionist. I was employed by the City from 1949 - 1991, starting at the entry level as a Public Health Nutritionist, then advancing to Supervising Nutritionist and ultimately to the top position as Director, the first and only non-medical to achieve this.

Other employment includes teaching and consulting: Instructor, New York Medical College, Hunter College, Newark Beth Israel Hospital, New York University, Cornell University, University of Iowa and Albert Einstein School of Medicine. Consultant, Head Start beginning in 1972 for Region II at New York University followed by the next 25 years as consultant for Region II at the National level, providing staff and parent training; Cornell University School of Human Ecology, New York Hospital School of Nursing, Pediatric Associate Program, Nutrition Research Advisory Council and Campbell Soup Company. From 1969-1972 I served on the Educational Advisory Council, National Livestock & Meat Board. In 1966 I was consultant with Institutional and School Marketing Department, Florida Citrus Commission, White House Nutrition Conferences and in 1969 a panel member and presenter. In 2000 I presented a paper, "Nutrition and Physical Fitness to Prevent Obesity."

From 1985 – 2012 served as Chairperson of Technical Panel on Nutrition (3 editions). I contributed to "Caring for Our Children," a compilation of health and safety performance standards for infants and children in-and-out of home care. It was published by the Academy of Pediatrics and the American Public Health Association. Yes, there were times I sensed I was being looked at as not being trained sufficiently to be in a position of Nutritionist. I took it in stride; the more others doubted my credentials, the more I did to excel. My inner strength gave me the courage to "think positive –this too shall pass!" As I look back some of those who questioned me ended being colleagues and offered assistance.

Awards I have received include the following: Fellow, New York Academy of Medicine, 1982 – present, Annual Catherine Cowell Public Health Nutrition Award by the American Public Health Association, Food and Nutrition Section to an Outstanding Public

Health Nutritionist, 1993 – present, First Distinguished Alumni Award, University of Connecticut, 1980, Outstanding Woman Employee, New York City Commission on Status of Women, 1982-1983, Public Service Award from the fund for City of New York, 1986, Public Health Nutrition Award, American Public Health Association, 1990, Ernest O. Melby Award, New York University, 1991, Excellence in Public Health Award – Quality of Work Life, New York City Department of Health, 1995.

Publications: co-authored with Simko M.D., Cowell C., and Gilbride, J. Nutrition Assessment: A Comprehensive Guide for Planning Intervention, 2nd ed. Rockville, MD: Aspen Systems Corp.,1995, Simko, M.D., Cowell, C., and Gilbride, J. Practical Nutrition: A Quick Reference for the Health Care Practitioner, Rockville, MD: Aspen Systems Corp, 1989. Twenty-three peer reviewed articles published in professional journals and eighteen published abstracts in a wide range of journals.

Presentations (International): 1975 Presented paper, "Infant Feeding Practices in Low-Income Families in New York City," International Congress on Nutrition, Kyoto, Japan. 1978 Presented paper at XI International Congress on Nutrition in Rio de Janeiro, Brazil, "Community Nutrition Source Materials – Recommended Nutrition Book List." Lectures and Workshops: From 1953 – present spoke to a wide range of professional and lay groups. One outstanding presentation was as guest speaker at the final graduating class of Dietetic Interns at Tuskegee Institute, Tuskegee, Alabama. Topic: "The Peripatetic Dietitian in the 20th Century."

Tips for the Legion of Well-Trained Professionals

ALWAYS BE YOURSELF! Prepare yourself well and avoid taking so-called "short cuts" or "cutting corners." In the long run, it doesn't pay because you usually spend more time trying to "cover" the deficiencies you thought you had avoided.

BELIEVE IN YOURSELF! Don't, however be "smug," thinking you know it all.

ALWAYS REACH BACK! Help bring them along. Grab the hand of another colleague and help bring them along.

Spritz
(Cookies)

½ cup softened butter
1 cup sugar
1 teaspoon baking powder
1 egg
1 teaspoon vanilla
3½ cups flour

Mix butter and sugar in large mixing bowl. Add baking powder and continue to beat mixture. Add egg to mixture and continue to beat until well mixed. Gradually add flour and mix well.

Press unchilled mixture into cookie press and place on an ungreased cookie sheet. Bake 8 to 10 minutes (or until cookie edges are slightly brown). Makes 90 pieces.

Nutrition Facts per serving (1 cookie)
Calories (kcal) 36.7

Fat 1.2 g
Saturated Fat 0.7 g
Trans Fat 0.1 g
Cholesterol 4.7 mg
Sodium 11.6 mg
Potassium 5.9 mg
Carbohydrate 5.7 g

Potato Fritters
(Using Left-Over Mashed Potatoes)

1 cup mashed potatoes
1 egg
4 tbsps. flour
½ tsp baking powder
1 tsp salt
¼ cup milk

Mix all ingredients together in a large bowl until well mixed. With a large spoon place mixture by spoonful into a hot skillet containing about ¼ inch of vegetable oil. When brown around the edges, turn fritters over and brown other side. Makes 10 fritters or about 4 servings.

Nutrition Facts per serving:
Calories (kcal) 98.9
Fat 2.2 g
Saturated Fat 0.9 g
Trans Fat 0.0 g
Cholesterol 45.0 mg
Sodium 802.6 mg
Potassium 197.8 mg
Carbohydrate 15.8 g

THE RELUCTANT DIETITIAN

Wilma Ardine L. Kirchhofer

From my earliest memory, I was going to attend college. In order to do this, I understood that I must excel in school. My father said, "You will have to do twice as much to get half the credit," and that became my goal. Mason City, Iowa had an African American population of less than one percent. My graduation class of 378 had four African American girls, and no boys. Nearing my high school graduation, the counselors said over and over, "the only field for you, a "colored" girl, is teaching or nursing," and that became my never-to-do goal! And that is how I eventually became the reluctant dietitian.

The Reluctant Dietitian

As I sat contemplating the annual dues for the American Dietetic Association, five years after my retirement from 'Corporate America,' I debated, "Shall I hold on to this Registered Dietitian designation for another year?" Who knows, I just may get a consulting job that requires an RD." I had to chuckle because for most of my 40-year career, I was reluctant to be a dietitian and here I was – seriously lamenting the act of giving up my RD status. After all, it meant something when proclaiming that I was a nutritionist or when I gave any dietary suggestions or even recommended a good meal, a restaurant or even a healthy recipe.

Being a registered dietitian said I was more than "just a cook," even though I consider myself an excellent cook and can be passionate about throwing a dinner party or experimenting with a new recipe. RD status gave knowledge, college, training and expertise to my love for food and nutrition. It means something very special to be a 'Registered Dietitian'. It is the ultimate authority on eating healthy.

Let me see; the reluctance began in high school, when I was first introduced to chemistry. I knew I wanted to be a chemist. Oh, I was fascinated with the concept that everything was created from molecules! And food was organic – just hydrocarbons. I wanted to create food substances that would allow one to be nourished without taking time out to shop, cook, and clean-up. No more washing dishes! My idea was just to pop a pill and dinner would be done!

My father quickly squelched the idea of my becoming a research chemist – "You would be competing with white men all throughout your career" – and he was the one to suggest a career path in foods and nutrition. "The curriculum is full of chemistry and the field is full of women." This was a time and a place when "fathers knew best."

Both mom and dad, Tressie and William Lyghtner, were born and raised in Iowa, both only children of parents who migrated from Arkansas and Tennessee; they knew the subtleties of racism and discrimination. Although the schools in Iowa were not segregated and Jim Crow was not sanctioned, the signs of separation were evident. We had black churches, one black professional (a podiatrist), one black restaurant (Mom and Dad's) and most of the men worked at the brick yard or the meat packing plant.

During my youth, however I enjoyed the fruits of a small Midwestern town: Girl Scouts, the YWCA, Baptist Training Union, 4-H and a host of neighborhood picnics, fishing trips, and barbeques. We traveled to other cities as far away as Des Moines, Minneapolis, Waterloo, and even Chicago to join African American clubs, organization, concerts and conferences. To get your "hair done" or purchase brown (not nude) hose, we traveled to Des Moines, home of my paternal grandparents. In our home, the Negro Digest and Black World were mandatory reading; and music was the albums from every living jazz artist known to man.

In the local Baptist Church, my public speaking skills were honed as we participated in statewide declaratory contests or memorized elaborate presentations for the Easter and Christmas programs. The length and complication of your 'piece' became your church badge of honor. And with the zeal to please my parents, I competed all the way to the top of the Baptist chain. Now I realize how important this practice in diction and delivery was to college and career success.

Growing up in Iowa, with limited exposure to African American life, my parents agreed to indulge my longing to attend a Historically Black College and University (HBCU). In Mason City, I always wondered, "Did I earn this or that award, or did they just want a token placement to show their tolerance?" There was a caveat to attending my choice of an HBCU, of course. I would return to Iowa State University (ISU) for the final two years – after all, in the words of Dad, "ISU has the best Foods & Nutrition Program in the world."

What better way to compete in their world – a degree from the best! So, I applied to several HBCUs and elected to attend Lincoln University in Jefferson City, Missouri. Note that this was the closest HBCU to my hometown in Iowa. As I departed for school, Dad had one last admonishment, "Don't you let me see you on television marching or demonstrating. "Just stay out of all of that. You are going to school to study, you hear?" And this was on the eve of the Civil Rights Movement.

So, I entered college in the Home Economics Department – that is where Foods and Nutrition was housed in the sixties. Yes, Dad was right, I could major in Foods & Nutrition and minor in Chemistry. This met my immediate desires, but career opportunities in the research world of food manipulation remained just a dream. It became clear that the career reality for an African American Woman in Food Science was going to be teaching dietetics or practicing dietetics – with an emphasis on hospital dietetics. I was about to accept a dreaded career of teaching or hospital dietetics.

One can see that my parents were the major influence on my life as a whole; forming my values, self-confidence, religious beliefs, and yes, my career choice. Growing up in northern Iowa, I was spared the rigors of segregation, but not the overt and covert acts of discrimination and prejudices. My parents continued to proclaim that I could be anything I could imagine and do anything that anyone else could do. Looking back, I see that the veto for a career in research chemistry was just to make my life a bit less stressful by minimizing contacts with racism and sexism.

Colleges, Universities and Home Economics

My experience at Lincoln University (LU) was more than I could have dreamed. It encompassed sorority; serving as president of the student government; desegregating the downtown shops and stores of the capital city, (without an appearance on television) and an engagement to the football team captain! Being a part of this HBCU elevated my feelings of self-worth and self- confidence. Admittedly, my Iowa education gave me a running start for academic success. This educational foundation led to the acceptance of my achievements as earned and not just patronizing.

LU was my first experience of African American teachers. The nurturing, the individual attention, and the encouragement given me at this HBCU linger with me to this day. These teachers set the standard for my teaching career later in life. The premise at Lincoln was to take it to the student, wherever you find him/her. Polish every stone into a gem. Everyone can learn, given the best encouragement and resources that a teacher can offer.

I maintain contact with the school, professors and many of my classmates to this day, some fifty-five years later. Both my sons attended LU for a year or two; and I even returned in the 80's to teach while completing a doctorate in Human Nutrition at nearby University of Missouri.

The summer before my sophomore year, I convinced my parents that Howard University in Washington D.C. had a chemistry course that LU did not offer – and this course would give me that needed edge to compete in job market. Quantitative/qualitative chemical analysis was my entrance to "The HBCU" that filled the pages of Ebony magazine and filled my dreams with African Americans in the health care professions. My lab partner for that summer remains my friend today. Fifty-five years, and we are still connecting through all the joys and storms of life.

I would have departed LU after my sophomore year, but as fate would have it, I was elected Vice President of the Student Government Association (SGA) and during the summer, the elected President announced he would not return. What father could deny his daughter such an experience – first female, and first Junior to hold the position of SGA President, But following this electrifying year leading the SGA through civil rights acts of sit- ins, marches, and unfortunately, expulsions for several students, and serving as Omega Sweetheart of the Omega Psi Phi Fraternity, I returned to ISU and began a marathon of classes. For five consecutive semesters, I carried the maximum class load and graduated just six months behind my LU class of '63 with a BS in Food Science.

It was at ISU that I got a taste of blatant discrimination. In my Journalism class, I continued to received C's or B- on my papers, and English composition had been on my A list at LU. It was just not making sense to me. So, a non-black classmate and I exchanged papers. She turned in my paper with her signature, and I turned in her paper with my signature. You guessed it! She got an A (on my writing) and I got the C (on her writing). Now it was clear. This professor was grading my work out of his own bias – discrimination without question.

When I discussed the recourse with my Dad and Mom, they agreed that I must pick my battles with care, and the opinion of this professor was not an indication of my writing skill. It was an elective, and I knew my skills were above average, so keep my eyes on the prize – graduation! There would be plenty battles against discrimination in the future, battles that could really make a difference in my life and my community.

Career Opportunity

While attending Lincoln University, I learned that my major in Food and Nutrition would eventually lead to the dietetics profession. I learned that the majority of jobs were in hospitals. My reluctance began growing again. I vowed not to teach or work in a hospital, but my path was headed in that direction. I learned that the military had great dietetic positions, but my brothers vetoed a military career for their sister, as did Dad. I headed the on-campus Peace Corp Club, but overseas "bush" life was out of conceivability for my conservative Iowa family.

After transferring to ISU, I was exposed to the many fields open to Food Science majors, other than Dietetics; communications, research, food companies, wellness programs, and on and on and on. A virtual gold mine of careers for Food Science majors!

So, when General Mills came to ISU campus to interview Engineering students, I signed up, equipped with my resume. The interviewer was surprised to have this Home Economics major at his table. I shared his surprise at my audacity, but asked that he take my resume to the Betty Crocker Test Kitchens (BCK) when he returned to General Mills. In less than a month, I had an interview with the director of the Betty Crocker Test Kitchens. I was flown to headquarters for an interview. The rest is history – my first job out of college – BCK, Golden Valley, MN.

What an experience! Home Economists were assigned a product line, i.e., cake mixes, snacks, flour. We followed our product from inception in the research laboratory, through market testing and on to public introduction. It required that we travel across the country for taste testing; make television appearances for product introductions; and develop recipes for an array of Betty Crocker Cookbooks. It was a dream job and it did not have hospital or classroom teaching in the description. Okay, I was not developing a pill substitute for daily meals, but I was developing a love for food preparation. And above all, without an internship or registration, I leveraged my degree in Food Science and Nutrition.

One of my early experiences with recipe development was the Impossible Pie. This was a pie without a crust, but during the baking the crust formed on top of the pie. I must have made two hundred variations before the final recipe was ready for publication. The recipe was kitchen tested, taste-tested, field tested, market tested, high altitude tested, and camera tested. Even today when I open a Betty Crocker Cookbook, I check to see if any versions of the Impossible Pie still exist. And sure enough, I still find this recipe today, 50 years after creation.

Betty Crocker...Impossible Cheeseburger Pie	Heat oven to 400°. Grease pie plate, 10x1½ inches. Cook and stir ground beef and onion over medium heat until beef is brown; drain. Stir in salt and pepper. Spread in plate. Beat milk, eggs and baking mix until smooth, 15 seconds in blender on high or 1 minute with hand beater. Pour into plate. Bake 25 minutes. Top with tomatoes; sprinkle with cheese. Bake until knife inserted in center comes out clean, 5 to 8 minutes longer. Cool 5 minutes. 6 servings; 420 calories per serving.
1 pound lean ground beef	
1 ½ cups chopped onion	
½ teaspoon salt	
¼ teaspoon pepper	
1½ cups low fat milk	
3 eggs	
¾ cups buttermilk baking mix	
2 tomatoes, sliced	
1 cup shredded Cheddar cheese (4 ounces)	

To Europe and back to Georgia

Being a Betty Crocker (BCK) home economist could have lasted forever, but I fell in love with an engineer from Switzerland and after five years with BCK, I married and began life as Frau Kirchhofer in the middle of Europe. As I look back, I do not recall any major encounters because we were an interracial couple in the '60s. The nation was in the midst of the civil rights protests for equal voting rights for black citizens and I was marrying a European and flying off to Switzerland. Yes, I remember the glances and the one person who refused to remain friends with us. But life in Iowa and then Minnesota was not a hot bed for Jim Crow or overt racial discrimination. Our life was inward focused where hate and distrust did not exist.

In Europe, we encountered more opposition to the war in Viet Nam than we did to the civil rights denied Blacks in America. Our personal conflict was more cultural. My husband did not want me to continue a professional career because none of the wives in his circle worked. When they did, it was done from the home--consultants, writers, painters, and even private practice medical doctors. I began to feel the loss of my identity and eventually this created the crack. What to do with my Food Science degree? I began to consult.

I would work with suppliers to place American products in the Swiss market place. Being in the center of Europe, I traveled frequently with my husband. I sought willing teachers in the best restaurants and spent hours in the best kitchens with the chefs. I perfected my German and even entered direct marketing of a California cosmetic line. The greatest achievement of life in Switzerland was the birth of our two sons, Gregory and Douglas. Once again, my career as a consultant permitted me to dodge the hospitals and classrooms. I was a very happy home economist, and a very busy mother of two.

This blissful life in Switzerland was not destined to last forever, and after seven years I found myself divorced and back in my homeland. Before returning, I researched the options thoroughly and decided that Atlanta, Georgia, had all the elements for a single parent with two preschool youth to move forward. The weather, the many universities, the diverse cultural climate, and it didn't hurt that Maynard Jackson was just elected mayor of the city. With the help of Lincoln University alumnae in Atlanta, I landed a position with Exodus Street Academy, a high school for youth unable to thrive in traditional school environments.

I was in a classroom – not at all food science but teaching and loving it! What a shock! The goal then became how to teach nutrition to the best of my ability and make a difference in the lives of my students. After a couple years with Exodus, honing my classroom skills, I was hired for a position with a grant-funded project to support elementary teachers in bringing health and nutrition concepts into their classroom. It was clear to me by now that teaching was the best schedule for single parenting. This allowed me to share holidays and summers with my boys.

During my time with the elementary school project, I enrolled in Emory University's Community Health Program in the School of Medicine. (This program later grew into the Rollins School of Public Health.) My Master's Thesis was a study of the relationship between eating behaviors and classroom performance of my elementary school youth. This area of study gave me contact with Georgia State University (GSU) and their program of Dietetics. It was during the latter part of my studies at Emory that I was encouraged by a professor to apply for an opening at GSU when I completed my work at Emory. By now, I was enamored with teaching and laughed out loud at my reluctance to be in the classroom.

ADA Registration Mandatory for College Teaching

Of course, a requirement for teaching dietetics program is to be a registered dietitian. This meant, in all likelihood I would be forced to intern in a hospital. What to do? At this time, the American Dietetic Association (ADA) was accepting Internships created and presented in a variety of sponsorships. I collaborated with the Director of DeKalb County Public Health Nutrition Service and my internship was designed, accepted by ADA and within the year completed. I took the registration examination and began teaching for GSU, as assistant professor in the Dietetics Program. Here I was, a registered dietitian, and in the classroom. The reluctance was behind me. For the next five years, I experienced a full range of dietetic relationships; professional organizations, friendships, mentoring opportunities and a growing love for the field of Dietetics. I had discovered that I could successfully continue my career in public health nutrition without clinical dietetics associated with hospitals. My focus became prevention of disease and the promotion of healthy lifestyle behaviors.

In academia, it is almost imperative to have the terminal degree to achieve full recognition. I began a yearlong search for a graduate school where I could pursue a terminal degree in nutrition. I avoided the schools that emphasized animal research. I did not want to nurture and then dissect anything; not mice, guinea pigs, chickens or any other animal used to study the influence of nutrients on health and disease. The fact was I wanted to study nutritional influences on humans.

Graduate School

One stop in my research for a graduate school was a visit to the Nutritionist working for The Coca-Cola Company in the area of Research and Development. She shared the particulars of the position and the curriculum she felt was most beneficial for a corporate setting in nutritional science. By the way, she was African American married to one of those Howard lawyers. Her position became the gold standard for my graduate school pursuit.

It was also necessary that I have employment during graduate studies as my middle school sons still needed to be fed. I settled on the University of Missouri in Columbia and found employment, teaching in the Home Economics Department, of Lincoln University, my alma mater. Between the two universities, I was able to put together a diverse committee that allowed me to use research facilities, and teaching opportunities at both schools. The research at Lincoln University (LU), was focused on nutrient utilization and international agricultural investigations. The University of Missouri (MU) was heavy on small animal research with international community relations. My committee agreed that I could do human nutrition studies in an international environment, but I would have to produce my own funding.

After several attempts, I successfully landed a grant from Agency for International Development to study the nutritional status in Upper Volta, West Africa (now known as Burkina Faso). I chose Upper Volta because both MU and LU had teams working there on other projects. My dissertation topic was accepted and I spent two summers studying the dietary intake of the population and then gathering samples of the "uncultivated vegetation" that was a large part of their diet. The one hundred samples from all areas of Upper Volta were gathered with the assistance of a Peace Corp volunteer. The samples were dried in Africa and transported back to the LU laboratories for nutritional analysis.

The dissertation was completed with a finding that showed the amino acid profiles of the uncultivated vegetation and the millet with which it was eaten, created complete protein. My graduate studies totaled five years, but so well worth the effort. The more knowledge I gained, the more I understood how much there was yet to be learned. Armed with a PhD in Human Nutrition with a minor in International Community Development, I was open and ready for a career challenge.

Corporate America Offers Career Option Again

Just months before my graduation from the UMO, I was recruited (another on campus visiting recruiter) by Ross Laboratories in Columbus, Ohio. I finished the final year of graduate school commuting between Missouri and Ohio. Both sons completed high school that year, so it was back to the 'Corporate America' working environment for me and college for the boys. During the five years in Missouri, can you believe, I let my RD registration lapse. Yes, I sat for the registration exam for the second time, as it definitely was a requirement for the position as Associate Medical Nutrition Educator at Ross Laboratories. The reluctant dietitian was back, but without any reluctance at this career juncture.

As one of several Associate Directors of Medical Nutritional Education at Ross (all with terminal degrees in nutrition) we developed and managed educational pieces for doctors, nurses, pharmacies and any end user of our nutritional products. Our product line was Similac, Ensure, Glucerna and other feeding supplements. Researching, composing, presenting and teaching were all aspects that I thoroughly enjoyed in this first career position following graduate school.

Most memorable was setting up weight loss clinics around the nation for a program system, that used Ross' New Directions – a liquid dietary supplement. This required in-depth collaboration with a diverse spectrum of the marketplace; physicians, colleges, and even realtors to secure space for our clinics. Client interaction came as we evaluated the effectiveness of the product and the weight loss system. Oh, I came close to that old high school dream of a food substitute when our staff tested this liquid dietary supplement for a week. It was clear to me that I loved the joy of eating and chewing food substances and the 'pill' approach was no longer my fantasy.

Working in the USA and internationally, there was very little overt or covert opposition to me as an African American in the workplace. One memorable occasion occurred when I was assigned to a project that required travel to a distant city, and the non-black male assigned to the project refused to travel with me, citing the possibility that someone might mistake us for more than business partners. I travelled, he did not. In general, my father was spot-on! I enjoyed a career in nutrition/dietetics with mostly women who neither opposed nor competed with me inordinately.

Ross was located in Columbus, Ohio, a hidden jewel city! It was filled with all the frills of metropolitan city (theatre, opera, art centers, university, etc.). Yet, it maintained a small town feel. I was settling-in with plans to stay a very long time when the call came from an Atlanta professor. She was aware of a position opening in Corporate America, a position for a PhD nutritionist with a background in academia, research and business.

You guessed it, the nutritionist I had interviewed six years previously had left the company. It took several attempts and several interviews to make the decision to leave Ross Laboratories after just one year. Finally, the offer was one I could not refuse; so ended my career experience with Ross Laboratories and I was hired by the Coca-Cola Company, headquartered in Atlanta.

My first assignment in the Scientific Regulatory Affairs department was to attend a Vitamin A conference in Ethiopia. Yes, the opportunity for international work in nutrition was a leading factor in my joining the company. Being a global corporation, we held memberships-- often founding memberships - in most of the organizations related to the ingredients used in our products. For example, sugar, caramel, vitamins and artificial sweeteners associations all have major input from our company. In addition, as the nutritionist I held memberships and active participation in most of the national nutrition organizations. The position met and exceeded all the aspirations I had for using my terminal degree. Would this be the final resting place for my career legacy?

As one finds in all corporate environments, there is an unwritten culture. A set of ways to be and not to be that were established and followed by anyone who desired to climb the corporate ladder. It was less than six months into my dream career that I realized I was not a 'fit' for the climb. It would require a sacrifice of me greater than I was willing to invest. I had just left an ideal work environment in Ohio to relocate to Atlanta, and I would not admit to myself or anyone else that this may have been less than a great decision. I steeled myself and determined that I would not leave this company. I would create another work situation that was the right fit.

Worksite Wellness – another Opportunity

One of my assignments in the Scientific Regulatory Affairs department was to consult with the Health Management Department – the area that conducted the wellness initiatives for the employees and their families. I convinced the department director that there was a need for a full-time nutritionist to support his program. I even agreed to develop and write the job description. Did you guess? I then applied and secured the position for myself. I became the Manager of Health Promotions for this department. Of course, it was not my intention to spend five years in pursuit of a doctoral degree in Human Nutrition and International Community Development to share office space behind the racquet ball court and dress daily in a warm-up suit. However, it was clearly a lesser sacrifice than what was required to continue in my current state of discontent.

As it turned out, the next twelve years were full of opportunities for creative public health initiatives for the employees, their families and the community. We often enlisted summer interns seeking degrees in exercise, wellness, and health management. Most interns were open to learning and gaining the needed experience to progress in their fields or enter graduate school programs. I delighted in this mentoring opportunity. We even had one intern from Iowa State University – and she was African American.

Although the Health Management Program was well known for facilities, exercise and fitness; the disease management program was in its infancy. We developed and implemented a Heart Rehab program for employees returning from heart attacks. The program grew and was recognized throughout the heart health community. In collaboration with our medical staff of nurses and a doctor, we were able to introduce allergy centers, lactation centers and travel medicine programs. Most of the disease management programs (hypertension, cholesterol-lowering, smoking cessation) were implemented manually. Today most are electronically delivered.

We had the opportunity to design these programs and implement these on-site using the tools we created. We began documenting our return on investment and after a few years could show a 5 to 1 return on prevention programs that impacted our health benefits cost. It was even more exciting when we could take our health management programs to the families of the employees and show additional cost savings through preventive services.

The years in health management were stress free, as we endeavored to create a stress-free environment at the workplace. We instituted health food lines in the cafeteria, stress management classes, tai chi and yoga opportunities, and a multitude of interdepartmental sports, competitions, weight management and health fairs. The disappointment always came when upper management would not value the dollars saved the same as they valued dollars earned. We saw many of our programs cut or dropped in each 'corporate downsizing.' Today, the entire health management program has been outsourced. Even the medical staff is managed from outside the company. Fortunately, my retirement came prior to the outsourcing of health management programs.

Encore Careers

Retirement coincided with my reconnection to my college fiancé. Although we had not seen one another for over 37 years, our reunion was sheer magic. We were transported back to the days when we were engaged at Lincoln University! We were both divorced, with children and grandchildren. In less than two years we were united; with the grandchildren giving us away at a family reunion and wedding.

He and I shared a passion for health promotion and disease prevention so we began a search for encore careers: FAO, CDC, WHO, and numerous national and international organizations that to us seemed a perfect match for our experiences, education and expertise. It soon became clear that the employers did not share our definition of a 'perfect match.' We concluded that the best way to make a difference in 'world health and disease prevention' was to educate youth to practice and promote health behaviors that prevent disease. Youth Leadership for Global Health (YLGH) was born. Together we researched, studied, created a framework, wrote a business plan, secured a 501(c)3, incorporated and launched YLGH, Inc. We wanted youth to understand that their health was in their control, and that they could make a difference. We believed that youth were the best peer educators and when given the right tools, they could change their health behaviors, and then go forward to influence the health of their families, friends, communities and one day the world.

To give our youth the understanding that health is a global issue, we added an International Health Study Tour to our program goals. Just days after 9/11/2001, our first Tour left for South Africa. Yes, we had the plane mostly to ourselves as flying was just beginning to recover following the tragic airplane attacks on our nation. We were amazed when the parents of our youth allowed them to continue with our plans, even saying, 'This is an experience of a lifetime. We cannot say no.'

In the fourteen years of directing YLGH, we touched an average of 150 youth annually. YLGH provided health education, leadership skills, mentors, and international health exposure. We were educating young leaders that would make a profound difference in global health.

YLGH groups were started in several states, and three countries. We were truly a global health education organization. Our Health Study Tours took us to South Africa, Ghana, Brazil, The British West

Indies, The Navajo Nation, Nicaragua and Cuba. We were honored with Community Service Awards from The Coca-Cola Alumni Association; Rollins School of Public Health & Goizueta School of Business. We captured the Social Entrepreneur Award from Hands on Atlanta, a Catalyst for Change Award from Pennsylvania, Champion of Hope Award from Africa's Children's Fund, and the Purpose Prize Fellowship for persons over 60 years of age who launch encore careers in areas of social need.

In all forty years of my career as a nutritionist/dietitian, the creation and management of Youth Leadership for Global Health is the legacy of which I am most proud. There is no reluctance, and no doubt in my heart and mind that my husband (deceased in 2009) and I were blessed to have this opportunity to interact with youth and fulfill our passion for nutrition and health promotion.

What is next? Family garners most of my attention. It is amazing to see my sons as fathers and husbands, and delightful to share in the growth and achievements of my grandchildren and great-grandson. Today, I continue to learn – oil painting and Spanish and any new software program that comes my way. It is international travel that really captures my imagination, allowing me to explore food cultures and geography of the world. My career as a dietitian opened the door for which I am eternally grateful.

FIVE WAYS TO BECOME A DIETITIAN NUTRITIONIST

*D*o you have a passion for health, food and helping people? A career in dietetics could be the right career choice for you. Becoming a registered dietitian nutritionist requires a science-heavy course load and many hours of patient care. There are opportunities to conduct research, work with children and even join the military. **RDNs work in a variety of settings** including clinical, business and management, private practice and culinary.

To become a registered dietitian nutritionist, a path of higher education is a must as well as a dietetic internship from an ACEND-accredited program, and passing the national registration examination. The pathway listed below is a common route many traditional students take, but it is not the only path to become an RDN.

The 5 Steps

1. Complete a bachelor's degree and receive a verification statement from an ACEND-accredited program (**Didactic Program in Dietetics**).

2. **Get matched** to an ACEND-accredited supervised practice **dietetic internship program** (some dietetic internships are combined with a master's degree, which is optional*). For students who do not match to an internship, applying to an **Individual Supervised Practice Pathway** is an option.
3. Pass the Commission on Dietetic Registration's dietetic **registration exam**.
4. Gain **licensure** in your state of practice, if applicable.
5. Maintain **continuing education**.

Other Pathways to Become an RDN

Coordinated Programs in Dietetics
Combine your degree with supervised practice. Why? Because baccalaureate students can apply to this type of program and begin supervised practice without going through dietetic internship computer matching. Coordinated Programs in Dietetics may result in a bachelor's, master's or doctoral degree, depending on the program. Graduates of these programs are eligible to sit for the dietetic registration exam.

Career Changers
It's never too late to make the switch to a career in dietetics. Individuals with a prior bachelor's degree need to complete a Didactic Program in Dietetics and receive a verification statement. Those without a four-year degree need to complete a bachelor's degree and receive a verification statement indicating completion of the didactic program in dietetics components prior to applying to the dietetic internship match.

International Students

RDNs have been trained in all corners of the globe. There a few different ways for international learners to become RDNs — visit **ACEND** to learn more.

Beginning in 2024, a minimum of a master's degree will be an eligibility requirement in order to take the CDR dietetic registration exam.

Academy of Nutrition and Dietetics

ABOUT THE AUTHORS

*I*n the unique work Six Eves Prevail through the Garden of Nutrition, six African-American nutrition professionals share their individual stories about becoming nutritionists and dietitians during the '60s and '70s. These professions have typically seen low numbers of African-Americans. The women whose stories make up this book formed close personal and professional associations that have lasted over decades. The book documents the mentoring, professional guidance, and wisdom they each received from trailblazers in their respective professions.

The importance of nutrition to the overall health of the population has been well documented. Though their career paths were different, each of these professional women made tremendous contributions to the health, wellbeing, and safety of their many patients, clients, students, and family members. Because of their backgrounds, they were able to bring a level of sensitivity to health care that was unsurpassed.

Narrated through first-person accounts, the book is filled with humorous and heart-warming anecdotes, personal and local history, recipes, and photographs. Journey with these special women along their remarkable paths that demonstrate the power of perseverance, the importance of family and community, and "lifting others as we are lifted."

Printed in the United States
By Bookmasters